Anna M. Fitch

The Loves Of Paul Fenly

Anna M. Fitch

The Loves Of Paul Fenly

ISBN/EAN: 9783744651868

Printed in Europe, USA, Canada, Australia, Japan

Cover: Foto ©ninafisch / pixelio.de

More available books at **www.hansebooks.com**

THE LOVES OF PAUL FENLY

BY

ANNA M. FITCH

G. P. PUTNAM'S SONS
NEW YORK LONDON
27 WEST TWENTY-THIRD ST. 24 BEDFORD ST., STRAND
The Knickerbocker Press
1893

COPYRIGHT, 1893, BY THOMAS FITCH
(*All Rights Reserved*)

Electrotyped, Printed and Bound by
The Knickerbocker Press, New York
G. P. Putnam's Sons

THE LOVES OF PAUL FENLY.

CANTO I.

I.

THERE 'S an isle in the sea—so the sailors declare—
So steeped in illusions of sublimate air,
That, viewed through the veil of the strange atmosphere,
All objects enlarged and illumined appear.
So shines through the mirage the ultimate West:
Its skies rain enchantment, the breezes are blest;
The sands flecked with silver, the rivers with gold;
Its atmosphere magnifies nature threefold;
The millionaire's million thrice multiplied seems,
And every man's fortune keeps pace with his dreams.
Its products outrival, (the flavor *n'importe,*)
Its trotters are bred to the fetlock—in short
Its grammar eschews each and every degree
Except the superlative.

II.

Ah! the *soirée*—
White satin and diamonds, *aigrette* in *coiffure*,
Gros grain and Brazilian bugs, train *de velour ;*
A beetle-wing watteau ; cascades *point de gaze ;*
Sea foam and pearl fringe, amber algæ in sprays ;
Cream velvet and marabouts, lace *à l'antique ;*
Sage green and swamp lilies, primrose *gros d'afrique ;*
An opal-hued satin, half smothered in tints,
Escaping from shadows and glints.—All devices
For fashioning altars for love's sacrifices.

III.

O woman! you waltz to the measures of wealth,
You smile on your hero, you sip to his health ;
You dote on your baubles, you chatter, and dance,
And languish in luxury—meanwhile, perchance,
He waits with mute lips, on some perilous brink,
Where sweep the dark waters of destiny—think !
The pleasures you covet, his peace may disturb ;
The exotic you choose, be his "diamonded herb" ;
You may barter his honor, and mortgage his pride,
Till, like drift on the beach left ashore by the tide,

The sun of society turns to decay
The flatteried fortunes itself swept away.

IV.

How easy to glide from the false to the true,
From diamonds and dreams to substantial *menu!*
From glimpses and glories and phantasy's play
To *pièce de résistance,* or *carte d'argent vrai!*
Some poet has writ of the difficult part
Of painting the lily, or detailing art;
But nature lies low at the nethermost roots
Of man's inspiration and impulse—the shoots
Are fashioned by accident, art, or perchance
As gas-jets in roses, or fountains in plants.

V.

To return to the supper; ah well, it is past,
Who lives for his palate, will hunger at last.
Confects in tall pyramids, palm trees in sweets,
Pomegranates in sugar, and melons in meats;
Epicurus and Bacchus, on kaolin vase,
A bust of Eratos—blue-belge for a base;
Lamp-holders in gems, candelabra in gold,
Tall vases in silver—acanthus-leaf mould;

Salons in mosaic, in agate and coral,
With frescos and paintings effusively moral ;
Oleander, magnolia, and jasmine in bloom,
Drift through the draped windows delicious perfume ;
While music and hours, in measure and tenses,
Stray out on the night wind, beguiling the senses.

VI.

When sorrow or ecstasy seize on the soul,
How fleeting, and flimsy, the scenes that control
Our commonest moods seem ; how straightway we seek
Dumb nature, unblaming, unblinded, yet meek,
Reposeful yet sleeping, though toiling untired,
No supplicant wooes her, but finds the desired
Response to his askings. The questioning shades
Of doubt or distrust, in the passionless glades,
Or the intrigueless solitude, waken a strain
As welcome as notes in a friendly refrain.

VII.

The time—date not named—of this same reception,
As shifted the midnight and smaller hours crept on,
A figure retreated, in *lisses* and *moiré*,
As figures will do when observed at a *soirée*,

Exceptionally and especially when
One's spirits are vexed or disturbed ; and again,
The effort to guess how one's features are playing,
Distracts the attention from what one is saying.

VIII.

To retire with grace,—half remain, half receding—
Is art of itself only gained by good breeding;
And, sad to relate, though the figure in *moiré*
Deported herself in good form at the *soirée*,
She elbowed her exit, inviting surprise
From the critical owners of critical eyes.

IX.

The night wind came languidly up from the west,
And the bay into tremulous dimples caressed ;
It played on the lawn, 'neath the high harvest moon,
And sung to the music in careless attune.
But the graceful adorer of "*moiré* and *lisse*,"
Who leaned on the bust of Silenus of Greece,
Was thinking of music, nor moon, nor the wind ;
Indeed, it is doubtful if erst he inclined
To such ruminations. A recent event
Had rippled the waves of his sumptuous content,

THE LOVES OF PAUL FENLY.

And now, while the dancers were merry within,
And none to observe, it was therefore no sin
To intrigue, or tryst—so thought Rupert Blondell,
The man of all men epicurean.—Well,
The rustle of drapery—his placid expression—
Are comments more potent than any digression.

X.

"Just why I have sought you here, Rupert Blondell,
Out under the cypress, I scarcely can tell;
For what I shall say, you will sagely conclude,
Might startle the ears of this chaste multitude,
If vaunted unwisely—unwittingly said,
Not otherwise.—Pardon me; is it well bred,
Albeit you rank as society's star,"
(He held in his fingers a guilty cigar,)
"To poison the air with no more perturbation
Than marks every act, for your own delectation?"

XI.

Miss Mora McBride had a resolute soul;
This attribute forges the key to her whole
Uncommon and many-hued destiny; born
To combat the rigors of fortune, the thorn,

Which sprang from the hard, impecunious soil
Of ceaseless endeavor and cankering toil,
Had entered the flesh, but to measure its length
With obstinate tendons of venomous strength.

XII.

If a resolute spirit but fixes its eye
On some pinnacled purpose sufficiently high
To shun the besetments that rise in the way—
The selfish allurements that lead it astray,—
'T will cleave every effort to fetter its wing,
And each aspiration its answer will bring;
As even the torch that the tempests outlast,
Is the torch borne aloft on the crest of the blast.

XIII.

Miss Mora McBride, as is often the case,
Succeeded in reaching the parvenu's place
In society's ranks, by simply ignoring
Significant glances, and smiles unadoring;
And measuring life by advantages gained,
She rarely relaxed till the end was attained.
The means were inconsequent; shrewd, without pride,
Her far-seeing vision acutely descried

The road to her object; albeit 't were strewn
With prayers, or reproaches, or terrors. As soon
The tiger, beguiled from his scent, turn away,
As Mora McBride from her well-chosen prey.
This unrefined woman, with consummate art,
Was playing a pulseless and passionless part;
The smile on her wide lip was dreary and dry,
And half-filtered gleams lit her beady black eye.
Her conquests diminished as years grew apace;
And memory, with some added lines on her face,
And a name not unsullied were all that remained
Of dreams unfulfilled, or a point unattained.

XIV.

On the Mediterranean, eastward from Nice—
The heart of her impulse, as Athens of Greece—
The traveller recalls, how a glittering vision
Invites the tired eye up the slopes of elysian
Delights; how the masses of marble and green—
With perfume and fountain and foliage between—
Look tenderly down on the tideless old sea,
And the dim, windless places that lie on the lea;
How up the broad terrace they tirelessly go,—
Old age and young maidenhood—thither and fro,

THE LOVES OF PAUL FENLY.

To deal with despair, both the timid and bold,
While their pulses keep time to the clink of the gold;
And yet, among all of the eager-faced train,
So hectic of cheek, and bewildered of brain,
Who madly defy all that fate can command,
On the turn of a wheel or the trick of a hand,
Not one played his game with more desperate will,
Or tangled his victim with readier skill,
Or treasured his triumphs with heartier pride,
Than she, the bold gamester—this Mora McBride.

XV.

Blondell was a man of the Jesuit type;
Unsound at the core, like a pear over-ripe.
He always a peared in the most approved styles,
Concealing his moods in the rarest of smiles.
Too bland for a cynic, too wise for a saint,
Too worldly for either, he scorned the restraint
Of laws artificial, though fixed by the same
Contrariotous world that he worshipped—the name
Of which, by the way, is Society—wherein
He sought to maintain his judicial bearing;
For, being a lawyer of greatest persistence,
'T was rightful to sift any law in existence.

His club and his freedom he vastly preferred,
Yet swayed with the weight of each fair woman's word ;
Repentant full soon, and too selfish, in sooth,
To tangle his life in the meshes of truth.
But of all that his enemies essayed to prove,
They never accused him of being in love.

XVI.

Fulfilling the office of simple narrator,
These latter remarks may have no *raison d'être*,
Any more than the actor, playing a part,
Should need to explain, or the artist his art
Should seek to elucidate ; still, in this man
Are found inconsistencies marring the plan
Of nature's sweet harmonies.
      Order and class,
In leaves of the forest, and blades of the grass,
Follow each uniformly, but may go astray
In man, as a melody loses its way
And wanders in chords in indefinite chime,
Yet, true to its musical numbers, keeps time.
What epicure was it, with senses so fine
That palled on his tastes were his viands and wine,
And fixed with a spirit of change in his diet,
Chose horseflesh to sate the unusual disquiet

Of cloyed appetite ? So this Rupert Blondell
With a world of refinement about him—Ah well ;
'T is a world of experiments. This is the lesson :
The act unæsthetic, we lay the least stress on.

XVII.

"Ah, madam, I know not which most to admire—
Your charming *ingénue*, or stately satire ;
The meeting is yours ; I am quite at your service,"
He said, with a smile that was wholly impervious.
The lady continued : "I wrote you a letter,"
He blandly retorted : "You should have known better ;—
Words spoken dissolve, like icicles in rain ;
But ink is a witness we challenge in vain."
She answered : "'T is true the words you have spoken
Are, like ice in your metaphor, easily broken ;
But let me assure you, without repartee,
The time has arrived when diplomacy
No longer avails ; I am fully aware
Of your dainty delay, and the ash your cigar
Reduces to frailness, the sport of your leisure,
Holds tenure as firmly as I, on your pleasure.
This night was the test ; in its scales I have thrown,
With desperate impulse, the Lydian stone

Of my fateful life. The result? I am dross
In crucibles social. But mark me! the loss
We will pocket together; you shall not escape,
Though Hades' broad portals were standing agape!
I am lost to society; lost is my life,
Unless you redeem me, and make me a wife."
"How long you 've been missing then, Mora, my dear"—
And his fine lip put on a perceptible sneer,
But the look on her face was so bitter and wan
That the gray marble stone he was leaning upon
Grew chill to his touch, and the shadows that fell
Seemed less apathetic than Rupert Blondell.

XVIII.

As she came, so *sub rosa* the lady returned,
Though her heart for his answer with eagerness burned.
He lifted his hat—'t was an "opera crush,"
Not required to conceal any possible flush,
For his face was as immobile, stony, and still
As the moonbeams that lie on a far distant hill.

XIX.

Oh, misguided woman; how blighted the sense
That sees in the world and its morbid pretence

Incentive more sweet and more subtle, supreme
Than dwells in the selfhood of woman ; ah, deem
The hypocrite's garb no less sinful than sin,
Or the panoplied purpose sincere, for the thin
And mocking devices of virtue it wears,
In disguise of the blemish it secretly bears.

XX.

"Unless you redeem me and make me a wife !"
These accents adhered, like a thing that had life,
To his brain. One by one, in obedient array,
He recalled and renewed them, then filed them away,
In the snug pigeon-holes of his mind, to await
The manœuvres of war, in the tactics of fate.

XXI.

Mad music, gay voices, confusion and din—
Wheels whirling without, and heads whirling within—
The banqueting done—the "good-nights" lightly said—
The guests and the glories together have sped.
But never a banquet or ball was there yet,
Where passion and pleasure together are met,
Where fancy, and fashion, and folly beguile
The judgment from soberer ways for the while,

But furnished some pivot—a pique or caprice—
For changing the motives of life, or its peace
Into pain ; and of all the regrets we recall,
How many bear date of some revel, or ball?

XXII.

For full half a month did Miss Mora McBride
Find consummate unction in nursing her pride.
Her moods, always moulded in equal degree
To man's adulation, habitually
Put by the subjunctive, assuring her friends,
That whatever the means, the substantial ends
Of her schemes were achieved. Her laughter was loud,
And her visage, uncoaxed by cosmetics, was plowed
With the unyielding lines of a purpose begun,
Or combats decided—not easily won.
Her secret she kept, taking counsel, in brief,
Of previous adventures which brought her to grief.
But of this, more anon ; enough for this story,
That plans for the future career of Miss Mora
Included Blondell—though, in sooth, she forgot
To reckon this item in casting her lot :
That love, like the creed of our best orthodoxy,
Embraces the scheme of salvation by proxy.

CANTO II.

I.

IN the difficult light, when the day is done,
   And the tawny fingers of night have begun
To twine in a love-knot the shadows and glints,
And tie them together with pale neutral tints
Of opal and amber and amethyst,
In a soft, uncertain, irresolute twist ;
When the gray lids fall on the dull, drowsy eyes
Of the sapphire sea, there will sometimes arise,
From the shrouding mists of the sepulchred west,
Like a taper new lit by a dead nun's breast,
A hurrying flame, as if worlds in their flight
" Might have lashed their dull steeds into flecks of light "
In their race with the sun.
                        Then the eager hills
Hold their ample laps, while the evening fills
Every darkening fold,—and the world below
Is immersed in one fathomless Afterglow.

II.

When passion and reason tend each to a side,
With paths so divergent, 't is hard to decide.
One leads by some Lethe, with lotus-lined heights
Of poplars, and myrtles, and wimpled delights ;
The other, through ice fields and stormy debris,
Invites to the open and infinite sea ;
And many the feet, like the trailing mimosa,
Get lost in the jungled "*via dolorosa.*"

III.

Not so with the hero of Mora ; he scans
With an eye self-serene his sufficient plans ;
He contemplates conjugal cares with a smile,
Relinquishing all speculations. Meanwhile
He remembers his vows, (though why should a woman
Beguile him of freedom in ways so inhuman ?)
His club and his comrades, his horses and hounds,
His cups and caresses, with all that redounds
To fame as a worldling—that sweetest of words
Which naught but the bachelor's license affords—
He holds indivisible, *sans* separation,
As scientists hold the monads of creation.

IV.

And so, in the light of the soft afterglow
Of the heavens above and the earth below,
This sage, philosophic adherent of Chitty
Walked over the hills that environ the city,
Past terrace, and garden, and lawn, and sand-dune,
And scented the flowers—for the wayside was strewn
With cool trailing arbutus, crisply entwined,
And violets breathing the sweet summer wind—
And solaced his soul with a certain design,
Which future events will best serve to define.

V.

For Rupert Blondell counted friends by the score,
And each in selection some relevance bore
To interests personal. "Friendships are well,
As serving one's purpose," quoth Rupert Blondell ;
And whether a song or a sermon, the measure
Of every man's worth must comport with *his* pleasure.

VI.

Contemplating, therefore, the list of his friends,
Computing the chances of gaining his ends,

Concealing the means, his artistic eye fell—
With wit not unworthy of Rupert Blondell—
On the sweetest of prey, one whom vulturous eyes
Of females who seek for some coveted prize
On the shoals of society, longed to impale
On fast fading charms.
     Also Mora, the frail
And care-fretted fabric of passion, began,
With the eye of the worldly-wise woman, to scan.
She quickly discerned this same self-saving spar,
While drifting away from her moorings afar;
This man of all men the most easy to win,
If only she knew where 't were wise to begin—
With his learning, his smiles, and his pale-brown locks,
His blandness, and gold, and his interest in stocks.
A stranger albeit—she received this with unction,
Such accident, leaving her free from compunction.
Her record—most students have vision contracted—
Looked best in a light just a little refracted;—
And wearied with hopes her hard fate to reform,
This prospect she hailed, as her port in a storm.

CANTO III.

I.

IF faces were fortunes, ay, verily then,
  Paul Fenly had been the most affluent of men ;
If ballads and oracles fitly combined,
Then blue eyes and dimples in truth are enshrined ;
But candor and constancy consort with grace,
Nor stamp their initials on any man's face ;
And many the serpent in wait to beguile,
Lies coiled in the mesh of a subtilized smile.
With a form that Adonis might envy, in truth,
This sweetly serene and ingenuous youth—
He was scarce five and twenty—won mighty applause,
For his accurate knowledge of hygienic laws.
Of life, and its mainsprings, relations, and rules :
A matriculate of the Heidelberg schools
Is sometimes the master of more than the arts
Of duelling, hazing, and love-making parts.

II.

When scarce more than twenty—the rumor was rife
Wherever he went—he had taken a wife
From his own lowly grade in society's strata ;
But subsequent changes had fixed an errata,
Where romance had ended and life had begun
In earnest. Indeed, he perceived that the one
He had taken to wife, for better for worse,
—Your pardon, O reader, if statements seem terse—
Had proven a plebeian. How wondrously wise
He had grown in these years ! But no need to disguise
That Paul was progressive. In his thérapeutique,
A repudiation, like pauses in music,
Gives zest to the movement.
                        But really we find
Too often the helpmeet comes lagging behind
In the rhythm of life.
                      Ah, woman, keep time ;
The high vantage-ground you may gain, if the rhyme
And step of ascent be of equal division—
But marriage demands such exceeding precision.

III.

For reasons like these had Paul Fenly declined
To fetter his feet with a weight. To the wind

His scruples he flung, and, as one may a gown,
He put by his wife like a garment outgrown.

IV.

This story is not one of sanctified folk,
Nor wherein the writer can hope to evoke
A soft sigh of sympathy. Patterns for youth
May be sought for in books less pretentious of truth ;
Yet candor compels the unwilling confession,
That sin seems more subtile till given expression ;
And molecules float as impalpable things
Unquickened by shapes, and unfurnished with wings,
But give them an animate presence, a note,
A plume, and a poise, and the air is afloat
With threnody, discord, chromatic or trill,
Ecstatic or sad, as the melody will.

V.

How truthful soever a record may seem,
The unwritten part is the better, I deem.
So therefore, "the cause why," the record of Paul
Showed deeds which politer interpreters call
" Intrigue," or "affairs," or some unmeaning name,
Which takes any signification, from fame

To infamy, just as society please,
—For all reputation is but a caprice—
Just why, to repeat, it were idle to question;
Sufficient that those whose best right to insist on
Some rendering, or writ of account, or negation,
Condoned all offences, and waived explanation,
As subsequent parts of this story will show
Those most interested conveniently do.
En passant—exhibit the scarlet of woman,
To vex social bulls to a fury inhuman.

VI.

Now sweetly embalmed in the wrappings of sighs,
And half-hidden tears from a hundred bright eyes,
The past of Paul Fenly is gladly resigned
To such lethean flow as his conscience may find.
By future events he may stand or may fall,
Faith shelters the few—Mercy covereth all.

VII.

Well panoplied now in his newly laid schemes,
And yet unaware that the rose-colored dreams
Of Mora had borrowed some prismatic glow
From his mind's bevelled glass, which marks the o'erflow

Of thought long accustomed to wander at will,
As marks water-cresses the course of the rill,
Blondell smote the clover that grew at his feet,
And murmuring some words 't were unwise to repeat,
He quickly returned as the daylight grew wan,
To keep an engagement with Paul, at the "Swan."

VIII.

Though quite unaccustomed to revel or riot,
Blondell sipped his wine in unusual quiet—
A fact which caused Fenly a little surprise,
For a sage must not needs be society-wise,
And Paul was a sage in his way, though untaught,
In lines which impel human motive and thought.
So therefore, when Rupert seemed *ennuyed* and bored,
Young Fenly was bland, and sincerely deplored
The state of his health, and averred, without question,
A glass of good cordial would aid his digestion.

IX.

Then straight laying anchor to windward, Blondell,
With true Machiavelian manœuvring, fell
On topics in range with his thought—if perchance
His plan he should forward, his projects enhance,

By luring the fancy, through soft lulling words,
To such eager heights as illusion affords.
He spoke—in the abstract—of womanly grace,
Adapting adroitly each figure and face
To Mora's. He modelled a character, too,
In eloquent phrase, as he artfully drew,
Fictitious or faithfully, qualities such
As while *en rapport*, not confronting too much
The sensuous eye of adventurous Paul,
Still captured his ardor, and held it in thrall.
Felicitous always, this artist had never
Made silhouette clearer, or sketches more clever;
And low in the depths of Paul Fenly's vain soul,
There burned the ambition his name to enroll
Alongside Blondell's; and with him to divide
The pastime of flirting with Mora McBride.

X.

The dinner concluded, each rose to depart;
And lighting a weed, with his hand on his heart
(In his overcoat pocket) Blondell made an oath,
That the charmer had virtues sufficient for both;
And friendship inspired him to offer with pride,
Next day to present him to Mora McBride.
Addendum. It argues the closest of ties,
To be able to see through another man's eyes.

XI.

"The greatest is charity," ponder them well,
These words that from lips sad and sinless, once fell
Like cool drops of water on fever-fed faces,
Or shadowy rocks, along wearisome places ;
"The greatest is charity " ; verily who
But needs all the charity earth can bestow ?
Whatever the act, whether wicked or wise,
The spirit of Mora's proposed compromise
With conscience, assuming that recrimination
Should furnish in some way self-justification,
She calmly proposed for her sins to atone,
By making another's accord with her own,—
A sort of *non sequitur* process ; but then,
Some women leave logic and ethics to men.
To her plaintive presumption, Blondell the astute
Gave quick acquiescence, and waiving dispute
About the exactness of Themis' scales,
With one side for women, the other for males,
They planned their first meeting with Fenly, and rested ;
All future conditions in destiny vested.

CANTO IV.

I.

TWO weeks; and Paul Fenly and Mora McBride
Had vowed each to each that, whatever betide,
The path of their future, through sunshine or tears,
—Less long for the bride by a number of years—
Should lie alongside, and within these few days,
—A fortnight's forever, when haply one plays
For a life stake—that each had delightedly learned,
How hollow the world, and how wholly it turned
On smiles and caresses, and that sort of thing,
And ended of course with a *trousseau* and ring.

II.

"No cards?" traitor thought; when the long march is do
When camp-fires are wasted, and battles are won;
When homeward the victor in triumph returns,

While hotly his thought with expectancy burns,
Who then should abandon—the roof-tree in sight—
The colors he won in the heat of the fight?
"No cards?" Opportunity gapes in amaze;
And social diplomacy's eyes are ablaze;
There were foes to be captured, and friends to be won,
Through prudent *finales* which chance had begun;
And policy, such as a pasteboard "at home,"
In fingers so cunning, so cool, and aplomb,
Was surely not used by this intriguing person
As means to convey either love or aversion;
But wisely as serpents, (not *et cetera*)
Proceeded Miss Mora with her *coup d'état*.
First came on the list, an array of the names
Of those who had lost in the lotteried games
Of "making a catch," in her own classic phrase—
Your pardon, some ladies have *prononcé* ways—
Then school-mates *passé* or unhappily wed,
A few nice young men, and a few underbred—
There were busy reporters, and traitors and friends,
All masking together to suit their own ends.
And finally, all—not excepting, in truth,
Nor sister, nor brother, nor friend of her youth—
All sneered as they smiled, while appeared side by side,
The names of Paul Fenly and Mora McBride.

III.

And prophecy saw, what the world wotted not :
How yielding the future, how hapless the lot
Of a woman aloof, who, with pivotless poise,
Seeks yielding support in those languishing joys,
That spring from such sordid, unhallowéd places,
As marital markets for loveless embraces.

IV.

The nuptials were done and forgotten ; the rent
On the sea of society closed ; the event—
The jeer of both club and *café* for the while,
Like yesterday's newspaper placed upon file—
O'erlapped by some subsequent scene or sensation,
Had finally ceased to invite speculation.
Meanwhile the ambitious, successful madame
More sweetly serene and self-righteous became ;
She patronized those whom she dared not ignore,
And placidly smiled on her patrons of yore.
All visiting cards with a notable name
Were placed in conspicuous places. The same
Ingenuous grace was bestowed upon those
Exceptional persons who annually chose

—And who could afford without loss of condition
Or quality caste—to make recognition
Of honest advance toward gaining those ends
Which ill-natured people call "making amends."
And if, as domestics were wont to recall,
She posed for "Madame" in the main servants hall,
'T were pity that Mora should e'er have survived
The innocent joys from such pastime derived.

CANTO V.

I.

How fares it with Fenly, his roots and his verbs,
   His clubs and flirtations, his billiards and herbs?
With face irresponsible, yielding, mobile,
With smile irresistibly sweet and facile,
With even a voice quite persuasively keyed
For passion or pity—to purr or to plead,—
He fully maintained his well earned reputation,
Of masking his moods with all imperturbation.

II.

Albeit he laughed with his scholarly guest,
As he tossed the Tokay with all manifest zest,
A clever observer would surely discern
The whitening smile, and the half-furtive turn
Of wide-open eyes, as the rustling gown,
Or the perfume of musk through the draperies blown,

Announced the approach of his wife. Yet of all
The casual comers who most valued Paul,
For rare contributions to their epicurean
Tastes, there was not among them, I am sure, one
Who saw through the mists of his own pampered sense
The causes which led to such subtle pretence
As Fenly essayed. So therefore 't will be better,
For reasons apparent, to scan his last letter
To one of his fellows, his old college mate ;
'T is simply transcribed without address or date.

III.

"Your letter received—many thanks—I am bored ;
Though how could you guess it ? I give you my word,
That when I wrote you, I had no such intention
As casting a mould for my moods, and I mention
The subject now even, because I 'm in doubt
Concerning how much of my secret is out.
'T is hard to comply with your modest request
To cancel my folly by making "clean breast"
Of subjects perplexing. One scarcely can stand
In the shadow one's self, and with master command
Compel the broad sunlight to sift the dark places,
Save only such space as *his* image embraces.

But we, my dear fellow, in bygones have had
Our innings together, for good or for bad.
My heart, if I have one, has opened to you,
And all it contains, be it false, be it true,
Is yours to command. Well, 't is something this wise :
You know what a marriage too hasty implies
In adage, and deed. But must it needs follow,
That projects unripe are all bound to be hollow ?
' Be off with the old ' is both honest and wise,
But since I am neither, why seek to disguise
The rather unsavory truth from my friend,
That where to begin, or wherever to end,
Has always perplexed, and so put me about,
And filled me with fears, that I 'm really in doubt,
If loves are not all—both the old and the new,
To take a reflex, Pythagorean view—
Some phantasmagoria, assuming new shapes,
As oysters are men, or as angels were apes.
But space will admonish, however I skirt
The uneasy edge of my subject, and flirt
With fancy or persiflage. One of my old
And chosen of charmers, with tresses of gold,
And eyes of deep sapphire—and that sort of thing,
You know how the rhymes of Anacreon ring—
Incited mayhap by some harrowing thought
Of vengeance—though she, I may note, too, had sought

Some alleviation in marriage withall—
One day at my rooms paid, *personné*, a call;
And there with those lips I had rapturously kissed
In days ante-nuptial, she fitfully hissed
Her shameless, unutterable, harrowing story,
Which, let it suffice, wholly scandalized Mora.
Now laugh, my good Carl, but pursue to the end.
This charmer—whose tale may kind Heaven forefend
I ever should question—had wisely provided
The proofs, which, however, discretion had chided
On every page, and in every line.
So amorous impulses always combine
With conscience, to check the precipitate part,
By charging the larger amount to the heart.
(*N.B.* Would you seek a base act to disprove,
Demurely declare yourself blindly in love.)
Now rational men would undoubtedly reason
Such marital statement must savor of treason;
So much I admit, only this would disprove
My course is exempt—I 'm not blindly in love.
Then why should I marry? Fate forges some fetters,
And hides the key in a bundle of letters.
Beside, too, our nuptials are half a year old,
And you, my dear fellow, need scarcely be told
How lucky I am to discover the link
In destiny's chain that is broken. Just think

How tame and unflavored this life would become,
With only the hackneyed accents of home,
And wife, and fidelity—all orthodox,—
But excuse me, your hand—I'm out of that box.
I've told you thus much of my story, dear Carl,
Unseeking your sympathy—really the snarl
Is quickly untangled, the one thing to meet
Is found in all circles, in salon or street.
'T is prejudice! You on that side of the world
Can well understand how a man may be hurled
From the Tarpeian heights of society's slopes,
By seeking to fashion the ground where he hopes
To stand, to his mind; for our marriage command,
Though based on an error as false as the sand,
Is, 'Thou shalt have no other gods before me,'
No matter how plainly perfidious may be
The god one is fatefully bound to; nor yet,
Was ever immunity found in regret.
This letter is long, and confessedly plain;
I'll be more myself when I write you again.
In truth, I propose to adopt the wise course,
Of drawing my draughts of delights from some source
Less poisonous. There is, I believe, on the Ganges,
A point, where the water its flow interchanges
With rivers unseen, and unmapped in the charts

Of all mortal delineators; the parts
At this ghostly junction, by Vishnu unblest,
Bring hapless disaster, and fill with unrest
The life of the man whose unfortunate zeal
Invites him to plunge in the waters that heal,
Unheeding the pious and mystical warning,
Or what is more sinful, its subtleties scorning.
I leave it with you, my old boy, to apply ;
And now for the nonce, your good health, and good-bye."

IV.

However untuneful, or out of accord
With congruous seeming these lines, they afford
A capable key to a character such,
As blameful, shall yet not be blamed overmuch.
With moral perceptions oblique at the best,
Paul Fenly saw life in the light of a test
Of human philosophies ; scorning the means
To attain, he declared, the reaper who gleans
The portion most large of the kernels of pleasure,
With less of the husks of contention, may measure
His life with the longest ; the fulness of years
Too often but proving the fulness of tears.

V.

A popular verse would be scarcely the place
Wherein to consider, with fairness or grace,
Those rare and phenomenal phases of mind
To which the unethical man is inclined.
Sufficient that Paul, with that warp of desires
Which fitly the soul of the subject inspires,
With more than the usual alertness, began
His course to retrace, without method or plan ;
Serene in the thought that, whatever betide,
He owed no allegiance to Mora McBride.
Nor cared that so finding the means of escape,
The doors of detraction went yawning agape ;
Not so with his friend, who was far the more wise,
Or cunning at least, as his letter implies :

VI.

"Your last just received ; what a consummate noodle,
To fiddle your national air Yankee Doodle
While other folks dance to some riotous rhythm
Your weakness induces. Not sympathy with them,
But cowardice, half of indifference, move
Your measures. Oh, bosh ! you were never in love.
Now take the advice of a friend—Architecture,
Of all arts exact, is the model. Your structure,

If reared on the sands of suspicion or doubt,
Must stand the derision of royster and rout;
Begin at the bottom, make certain foundation,
Then follow your purpose, without perturbation;
In treating a malady, scan all the signs,
And symptom the case, as you sample your wines,
By questioning steps, and precautioned removes,
Through highly bred flavors, and deeply laid grooves;
And be sure the *a posteriori* logician
May seize a sequence with extremest precision.
More plainly, if too hypothetic my plan,
Initiate movements by 'spotting your man,'
Quite mindful that best you his faith may beguile,
By some confidential assumptions the while,
Respecting yourself and your half-revealed story,
With some semi-certain allusions to Mora.
'T would not be unlike you, in order to shirk
These politic details, to bungle your work;
But let me forewarn you, unless you succeed
In proving your marriage a fraud, you indeed
Provoke such decree as no law may exempt,
The surfeited victim of common contempt."

VII.

And this was not all of this mettlesome missive,
But let it suffice, for only we this give,

To show how the venturous risk their advice,
As the schemer his plot, or the gamester his dice,
On the green cloth of Fate, without stanchion or stay,
To those who but estimate life as a play.

VIII.

Paul Fenly was puzzled ; the way was not plain,
—Ways always are dim, 't wixt the morals and brain—
And science fell short before ethics began,
Thus leaving a lapse between scholar and man.
However, this learnéd compounder of potions,
Though strongly inclining toward his own notions,
Began to discern that, whatever his will,
He surely had swallowed another man's pill ;
So straight making such therapeutics the rule,
As fairly pertain to the Hahnemann school,
He promptly proceeded his nausea to smother,
By treating one dose of disgust with another.

CANTO VI.

I.

THE gray mists swung down by the low-sounding shore,
  And frosty-lipped surf bit the sands on the floor
Of the unsheltered beach ; the blue windy hills,
Keeping watch over shoulder and shroud as it fills
In the face of the gale, held their breath in amaze,
As the storm combed their temples with roughening ways,
Down over the sea. Up the querulous street,
With meddlesome, quizzing, and hurrying feet,
It ambled, and swaggered, and chattered along,
Now wandering wayward, now mixed with the throng ;
Unconscious, uncaring, unconquered it went,
Till the last beating breath of the storm was spent.

II.

'T was just such a morning that Fenly elected
To visit Blondell, and though quite unexpected

To Rupert, he put on a face like a ritual,
For, noting those ways not in Fenly habitual,
He took his first bearings ere Paul had a chance
His preliminary pickets to advance.
" Your time "—Fenly spoke; quoth Blondell—" is my own ; "
There was something sententious and dry in the tone,
As crossing the floor, he wheeled over a chair,
And lazily offered a fragrant cigar.
Both sat, and some moments quite laggingly ran,
Till finally Paul cleared his throat, and began :

III.

" I 've come with another man's proofs, don't you see,
So all inadaptedness rests upon me.
It may be the man has o'erstated his case,
In such an event 't is our business to trace
The facts to the diverging point, don't you see ?
And sift out suspicions, or make them agree."

IV.

Blondell did not see, but he looked wondrous wise,
With his low-drooping lids, and his semi-closed eyes ;
Then winked in a half-bored, leisurely fashion,
As lawyers will do, when some question they pass on.

"Observe," argued Paul with unusual aplomb,
Now grown with his counsel and case more at home,
"The only one duped in this novel transaction
Is he, whose good faith we must draw all our facts from.
Society, seeing their votary's plight,
Betook to their pinions, and made hasty flight,
Especially those—you have witnessed such things—
Who, wounded themselves, bore the shafts in their wings."
"Now I see," answered Rupert, "our client's a fool;"
And he shifted his seat in his sumptuous *fauteuil*.
Paul laughed in a high, half-uncertain falsetto,
But quickly resumed his disordered libretto,
And followed with speech hypothetic, while we
Have followed more closely the story *per se*.
"The wife," pursued Fenly, "is yet unaware;
Maintaining unchallenged, her fine debonair."
"Our client's a coward," quoth Rupert, in haste,
"And poorly deserves the defence which you waste—"
Here Paul interposed—"But the man is, alas!
Half maddened"—quoth Rupert, "Our client's an ass."
Then Fenly rose up for the last *coup d'état*,
While Rupert exploded a syllabic, "Bah!"
One effort, and Paul must succumb to the "bluff,"
Albeit of proof he had amply enough
In Rupert's affected and *blasé* demeanor,
But how to entrap this ineffable schemer

Was surely an end not obtained by convictions,
And for strangling men, he had no predilections.
"Perhaps I neglected to mention one clew
Of evidence ; merely to satisfy you,
I 'll add that the letters sufficiently plain,
Which fell in the hands of our client, remain,
To show with what ready and genuine skill
A man may contrive his caprice to fulfil."

v.

Now here was occasion for tactics—no crude
Or unrevised statement, however imbued
With logic, could capably cover the ground,
Whereon new reprisals might tend to abound.
Paul, turning to Rupert, looked full in his face ;
'T was simple, sufficient, with never a trace
Of change, or alertness, or conscious surprise,
Save only a dreaminess crept in his eyes,
Enshackled a moment, and held them in bay,
As fast speeding steeds, when a cloud breaks away,
And flashes of light unaccustomed reveals
Weird scenes, such as nature, unsuaded, conceals,
Get back on their haunches, defiant nor daunted,
But seized by some swift speculation, enchanted.

VI.

'T was but for an instant, and Paul no adept ;
But into his hiddenmost instinct there crept
A swift revelation, dim and evasive,
But high above pleadings and verdicts persuasive.
It sat at his hearthstone and supped in his brain,
And never gave respite or ransom again.
Take note ! it was only vainglorious pride
That felt the fine treachery of Mora McBride,
And when he departed, he cherished no grief
That investigation sustained his belief.

VII.

For Rupert Blondell, whatsoever ensued
It must be confessed that his "method" was good.
The cleverest artist may err in his sketch :
In painting a distance, expanse may outstretch,
Or, losing a moment the reckoning line
Of vision, may slightly refract the design ;
Exactly how Rupert deflected was this :
Though nothing in form or in color remiss,
He o'erlapped the margin by trying his tints,
His pigments and brushes, thus leaving some hints,
Some signs which betrayed the *modus operandi*,
And which for best reasons he cared not to stand by.

VIII.

'T is wonder, when life is reduced to a scroll,
When big with their travail, the Heav'ns shall unroll,
When books shall be opened, and actions undid,
And hearts and intents can no longer be hid,
If errors and crimes shall be found to have sexes,
And whether the question of gender perplexes
Savants of the higher and ultimate school,
So far—as with earthlings—as quite to control
All edicts and verdicts, or if they define
Transgression as masculine, sin feminine?
Let those who can answer, still further decide
The odds between Rupert and Mora McBride.

IX.

Months wasted, and Fenly still smilingly went
From under the roof of his heart's discontent:
Went forth among men, and as smilingly came,
As if he had gained his most coveted aim.
But e'en as the pulsings of Nature express
Recoil and advance, as her means to progress,
So Paul's retroactive conditions asserted
A law of his life, never yet controverted,
That loves, like the tides, have their ebbings and flow,
As billows well spent mark some strong undertow.

CANTO VII.

I.

HIGH noon in the suburbs one morning in May !
  The tones of the Angelus slipping away,
Dropped down, one by one, on the matinal air,
Like telling of beads, or the patter of prayer.
The lawns of the nunnery *de Notre Dame*
Put by their dull role of habitual calm,
And vocal with notes of their annual chime,
Blent color or chord in harmonious rhyme ;
And corridor, court, and pavilion were rife
With the jubilant glow of young animate life.

II.

Fast gathered the throng from afar and anear ;
Fast crowded each vestibule, porch, and parterre.
The chapel, afloat with translucent attires,
Forgot the dusk prose of the old vestal fires,
And honeys swung out on the ambient air,
More subtile than incense, than spices more rare

Than ever from censer or petal were blown,
Or chemist distilled. On the cool marble stone
Of shrine and of chancel, young maidenhood knelt
One moment in prayer. Such grace as might melt
The adamant heart of that ground, doubly blest,
Bowed there in the unstarry stillness of rest
And pious repose ; and then lifting the cheek,
Like lilies half blown in the moonlight, the meek,
Soulful and sufficient, completely poised Nun,
Kissed lightly, with passionless lip, one by one,
Each maid as she passed her in loving review,
As snow-flakes fall softly on roses and dew.

III.

A stir, then a rush, and the screen rolled away,
Like many another on festival day,
And summery skies and a tropical sea
And shadowy ways pictured old Galilee.
A chorus of voices as fresh as the breeze
That stirs the young leaf as it leaps from the trees
Made echo, like musical birds in the boughs
When life is one song, in one ecstasy flows ;
Then fast fled the fairy-like forms to the vale,
And all the strong melody blent in one wail,
From lips that were wet with the virginal dews
Of young inspiration.

IV.

More fully the Muse
Holds converse serene with religious sense,
And haply more potent that, shorn of pretence,
This maiden abandoned her self-thoughtful ways,
And yielded her power to pray'r and to praise.
When therefore in meek invocation she bowed,
A shaft of the sun, from the rift in a cloud,
Fell deftly aslant on the sanctified place,
And so reillumined the pictured young face,
As kneeling, she clasped her slight fingers in air,
While aureate lights fell among the bright hair,
And dropped into tints in the shadow of pearls,
And draperied crape, like the sinuous curls
Of water, moon-lit as it laps round the stems
Of lilies half bent, half erect; while the gems
Of white far-off stars set their stilly repeat
On eyes turned to Heaven, that holiest retreat.

V.

The prayer changed in rhythm, and "Father forgive"
Slid fast into numbers of recitative;
The songstress stood up, and the light which had gilded
Her features gave way to an ecstasy, builded

Of passionate fires, that illumined the theme,
And justified faith in adopting the scheme,
Which somewhat entangles the way to salvation,
But which one accepts as one should revelation.

VI.

Albeit Paul Fenly, in music inapt,
In fulness of soft delectation sat wrapped
As round with a garment new-made, for a spell
Of feeling, half awesome, half rapturous fell
On heart and on brain, and for one single hour
He yielded his soul to the sources of power
Not generic here in the flesh. In a word,
He worshipped in spirit the name of the Lord.

VII.

A sensuous mind some religion may thrill,
But a sensuous eye only woman can fill ;
And Paul's was a nature compounding the whole
Voluptuous sense, with a worshipful soul.

VIII.

As winds from the west, down the wet meadows blow,
When the sun is at rest and the weak moon lies low,

So wandered the strains like a spirit half lost,
Now torn by fresh sorrows, now hopelessly tossed
On waves of unrest, or low-lying complaint,
Yet seeking some goal ere the spirit should faint;
But e'en while the lax and attenuate tone
Sank low in the soul, and seemed lost in a moan,
A kindling chord and a new-found refrain
Stirred the ash of despair into embers again;
And the uprising impulse, the absolute beat
Of baton peremptory, short and complete,
Revested the spirit, emboldened the heart,
Impassioned the motive, and realized art,
Till passion and pathos so actual became,
That all the vast audience broke forth in acclaim
And rapturous applause, while the anthem of praise,
With gathering power and in holiest phrase,
Uprose with the tramp of a host battle-shod,
And the oracle bore to the gates of God.

IX.

The maid with the aureate lights in her hair,
Undreaming her triumph should serve to ensnare
The too willing thought of a listener, smiled
A smile soft and special, but one which beguiled

With rhapsodic dreams the remembrance of Paul,
Who, after long seasons, was wont to recall
The roseate hues of this scene from the past,
Like one single star when the skies are o'ercast.

x.

When Augusts are ended, and autumn suns shine
Through vari-hued boskage and crimsoning vine,
A little brown workman comes out of the haze,
With soul of deceit, yet with softest of ways,
And clad to the eye in some levelling shade
Of russet and gray, he proceeds to invade
The sacredest forest with armies of schemes
Of fine spun illusions, as subtile as dreams,
For entangling some feeble and unwary wing
In meshes as fateful as mirage.   Then bring
The metaphor home, and apply it to Paul,
" It is old "—so is art.   Truth rejuvenates all.

CANTO VIII.

I.

IF Love were a spark from the Infinite fires,
   Enkindled by glintings of mortal desires,
As poets have written, what conflict of force
Dissuaded the impulse from poise in its course?
What power interposed to impel it astray,
Or lined with illusions its devious way?
What sophist, with artful and cunning conceit,
Contrived the stout logic of truth to defeat,
Through gloried beguilement, or sensuous spell,
Through faith in false idols—through lives that rebel?

II.

Sweet Sappho! poor heart! all Leucadia sobbed,
And hamlet and street with the threnody throbbed,
As, silenced the melody, shattered the string,
The pain in her breast, and the shaft in her wing,
She sang her despair to a listening world,
And fashioned her bed where the dark waters swirled;

But never a Sappho the less, nor a moan
For memory of Sappho, the less, by a tone.

III.

One day in December, close down by the sea
That washes the sands in its sensuous glee,
The stout-hearted lupin and fuchias maroon,
All purple and red, filled the white afternoon
With perfumes and colors of various degree,
This day in December, close down by the sea.
The ocean that rocked in the lap of the wind
Had forged the huge key for th' Orient and Ind,
And while on its watery hinges there whirled,
The gate that gave welcome to half of the world,
No fettering frosts, or snow-stiffening gale,
Or icy-bound breath, ever sat in a sail
That shadowed these waters, or sipped of the breeze,
Or fled at the tramp of a storm on the seas ;
So kindly the airs on this sun-pampered shore,
So passion-provoking—with love so *rapport*—
One day in December—'t were well to begin
If only to show how much love looks like sin.

IV.

The winds had upbuilded a sea-wall of spray,
Lashed up from spent tempests one memorable day,

The swell of the billows, the voicing of waves,
The shrill, well-known cry from the far ocean caves,
That beat like a bell, or a funeral tune
When swept by the wind—whether midnight or noon—
Belabored the air with familiar refrain,
And faithfully told of the storm on the main
With telephone wit. The sands on the beach
Were scarcely more countless, so far as could reach
The vision to landward, more impotent, too,
Than human endeavors to capture the view
That Nature's broad gallery donated free,
This day in December, close down by the sea.

v.

Along the broad pave just where sand-dunes divide
The heights from the lowlands, caressed by the tide,
Paul Fenly, with mount of *Chevalier*, and grace
That well matched the smile on his flexible face,
Rode dreamily on through the sunshine and sheen,
Which fell through the boughs, with the leaves, on the green
And fresh blooming banks, though the day was December
—Unless well reminded one scarce would remember.
Alas! it were well if the world could forget
That just at this turning Paul Fenly had met
Once more the quick glance of the steel-purple eye
Of Persia, the maid of the song and the cry;

Or that, in so meeting, he paused with a gesture
Albeit unstudied, had startled, impressed her,
And brought to her face, quite reposeful and still
Of habit, when stirred nor by passion nor will,
A look half of hauteur and half of alarm,
And all of forgiveness—one wholly *du charme*,
Then sank in the cushions, and wondered, while he,
His thought with the girl, and his eye on the sea,
Set spurs to his steed, but confirming the while
The dimples defining the depth of his smile.

VI.

If cause and effect should more closely relate,
Then Prudence might cunningly circumvent Fate.
But causes most rational lead to refraction,
And sequences follow too late for retraction.
" If ne'er we had met " has been writ in the doom
Of loves that were blighted since Eden's first bloom
Dropped fruits that were withered ; so wrong follows right ;
If never a bud, there were never a blight.

. . . .

VII.

A scent of fresh violets fell on the air,
And vapory perfumes of dank maidenhair,

Half-wood and half-swamp, led the senses away,
To meadowy places, where cool waters play
Along the green banks.   Then the pausing of wheels
Called back the stray thoughts from the fanciful fields,
To a lithe little figure, scarce more than a child,
As fresh as the scents that this moment beguiled
The fancy.   Draped soft, as the breast of a dove,
In shades of the flowers she held in her glove,
She swept up the marbled and ebonied hall,
And smiled in the welcome of Mora and Paul.

VIII.

Ah, Persia, why heed not the oracle's voice,
Which whispers each soul that is granted the choice
Of ways that are doubtful?   What witcheried spell
Entices thy feet through these portals?   As well
Seek aureoled Hope in the caves of Despair,
As for peace in this dwelling.   O Persia, Beware!

IX.

For Mora, with all the far-seeing acumen
Attaching by right to the worldly-wise woman,
Quite conscious that ever since Lucifer fell,
" The better has still been the foe of the well,"

Yet challenged the proverb to meet such a need
As seemed to confront her at present ; indeed,
She clearly foresaw, if she hoped to constrain
The volatile movements of Paul, she must gain
Some element foreign, some sunshine and birds ;
Some ideal pictures ; some songs without words.—
Society thus its thinned ranks reinforces,
And brings, to replenish depleted resources,
The fledgling new-loosed on the half-opened spring,
The down on its breast and the dew on its wing ;
No matter—if pleasure shall gain by a note—
That voiceless it die, with the song in its throat.

x.

So Persia, not quite seventeen, nor yet "oút,"
—That slang is expressive no critic can doubt—
Beguiled by "informals," or "Ah ! Apropos,"
Or "only a friend or two," "never *de trop*,"
With sometimes a "Musicale," "German," "Quadrille,"
And frequent engagements to dine *en famille*,
Came lastly to look in Paul Fenly's blue eye,
Some day in each week, without questioning why,
And then to her maidenly conscience confessed
That, scanning the list of her friends, she loved best
The one who—she cared nor for prestige nor story—
Made earth Paradise ; and that woman was Mora.

CANTO IX.

I.

How many a happ'ning—how many a face
  We glimpse for a moment, then lose every trace,
When, lo! it recurs, not more present or real
Than that which we saw just now in ideal!
The gift we call prescience—the going before
All science and knowledge, to open the door
By faith to conviction;—the thoughts that impel
Strange fathomless reckonings, oftentimes tell
Their voiceless oracular way to the gate
Of events—in a word, they anticipate fate.

II.

And thus it transpired in the course of this story;
The reaching suspicions which overtook Mora,
Gave fashion and moulding to subsequent schemes,
Which, left to themselves, might have ended in dreams.
So lapse of events, with means still more subtile
Developed effects beneath Destiny's shuttle,

That startled the maid into livid surprise,
As, bearing her burden of grief in her eyes,
She sought unprotected the presence of Paul,
And low, and with trembling, rehearsed to him all
The mischievous slander.
     What answered the man?
In phrases as old as the world he began
By probing the wound of his own discontent;
"The woman did tempt me"; what years he had spent
In futile and useless endeavors to mend
A fracture to faith! There were faults without end
Of conscience, and temper, and taste; there was scorn
To heap on her head for the child that was born
Of nuptials so wholly perfidious. As soon
Seek figs among thistles, or stars at high noon,
As fruits that were wholesome or sweet to the taste
In ashes, or marshes, or places laid waste,
By passion withdrawn. All ambitious pursuit
And purpose lay prostrate, or latent or mute,
In view of this horror. Till late he had never
One thought entertained of a nature to sever
These odious bands; was it strictly in duty
To bury his life from all brightness and beauty,
Away in a sepulchre, snow-girt and frozen?
(That day Mora reckoned his amours a dozen)
If so, he must bear and be patient the while,
Though stricken of soul he would suffer and smile,

As hot with disdain, yet defiantly dumb,
He wait till the day of his destiny come.

III.

Now Persia had listened with dilating eyes;
Forgetful already, of half her unwise
And witless behavior—in making selection
Of one to entrust, whose peculiar objection
To Mora seemed based on some personal wrong
Too stale for a story, too tame for a song—
Her fancy-fed feeling made ample excuse
For all his wild outburst; the delicate truce
To slander, implied by his non-recognition
Of threatful aspersion, and subtile suspicion,
She fancied a merciful foil to the force
Of blows which he hoped to distract from their course.
Thus warped in the grain of her innocent trust,
By unalert judgment, all subsequence must,
In deed and in purpose, bear date of the hour
When Persia, o'ermatched in the mystical power
To rend or resist, as the current may will,
Unwittingly yielded her heart to a thrill
Of sudden-born sympathy.
      Strangely akin
Are pity and passion, as love is to sin.

IV.

As follows the fever a languid content,
Or a calm when the strength of the tempest is spent,
As rhythm succeeds some unmetred expression,
Or restful relapse the erratic digression;
As world-blown, the bird flutters back to the nest,
And stretches its limbs in unhazardous rest,
As forth from the mesh of some tangling eclipse
The newly bleached moon, half regenerate, slips
To fields twice more fond and familiar for aye,
For the nightly march, and the shadows gone by,
So Persia, that night, like a fawn to her lair,
So graceful of limb, and so shining her hair,
Escaped from the swaying contentious throng,
And sought her own chamber.
     Reposeful among
The floss-fashioned daisies refreshing her bed,
She quickly found rest for the weary young head,
But sleep long delayed.
     Not less white than her peer,
The moonlight, nor radiant of feature, the clear
And unveilèd eyes caught aflame in the light
And trebled their lustre.
     Abroad on the night,
The child looked and languished; some far-off regret,

Half pain, half contentment, a feeling not yet
Undid from the swaddlings, stirred first at the heart,
Then fled to the brain and made parcel and part
Of thought ; 't was the welcome and privileged guest,
Named Sympathy, asking for lodgment and rest
In the name of Paul Fenly ; what had her young soul
To do with the trickster's intent to control
Her heart's best emotions ?
      Ah, better this night,
Her beautiful feet should lay hold on the white
Evanishing road of eternal decree,
Than walk in the mire of the years yet to be.

v.

Albeit the girl from her sumptuous height
Of maiden reserve and reluctance, this night
Framed fanciful speech to a phantom array
Of auditors met—in her mind—to gainsay
Her prudence in lending an ear to the plea
Of Paul, and his doubtful defences, yet she,
A prayer on her lips and a cross in her hand,
Made haste all her harrowing thoughts to disband ;
And then without caution, or counselling word,
Or only by angels of grace overheard,
She wrote with warm lips, on the starlight alone,
The iciest vow to the human heart known,

That—never so tempted—should earthly born love
Her heart render captive, her reason disprove,
As worlds were to witness!—She saw not that Venus,
That moment slid down in its orbit between us
And soberer lights. Then she finished her schemes
In ways quite peculiar to regions of dreams.

VI.

Meanwhile, Fenly smiled in his sunniest fashion,
And nobody knew if in peace or in passion
He caught from the purplest wing of the night,
Some plumes to upbear in their venturesome flight
Those messages earth-born but heavenward tending—
As commonest lives may have luminate ending.
Sufficient that Mora, with cunningest scorn,
Of vanity bred, and of jealousy born
Instinct with discernment, as one self-convicted,
Will ferret a foible from ways interdicted,
Eschewed, unsplenetic, his sullen-pent passion,
And coolly proceeded suspicion to fasten
On Persia, by means which a proverb has made
Quite lawful; in love as in war it is said,
All measures are fair; when therefore the lady,
With trickeried fingers and ways that were shady,
Discovered some secret and sacred recess,
On whose dark retiracy Paul laid much stress,

'T was plain that whatever the means she employed
It signified nothing with that she enjoyed
Of exquisite anger, and tortuous bliss,
In bringing to light and disloyalty this
Bare, bald confirmation—this grip to her wrath,
This proof of defiance of conjugal faith.
'T were well if Paul Fenly in verses had spent
Like many a lover his heart's discontent ;
'T were better that e'en on some Tantalus lyre
His over-matched nature should writhe and expire
In sensuous rhymes, such as these he essayed
With pencil and parchment to Persia the maid.

VII.

But violence done to her marital pride,
Ill-suited the measure : the name of McBride
Affixed to some letters of much prior date,
And long since forgotten, 't is strange to relate,
Attesting the truth of the troublesome story
Which long ago ceased to intrepidate Mora,
Believing in Rupert somewhat, and still more
His word that "the thing" was a "consummate bore."
The name, to repeat, on the letters in question,
In her own handwriting, in Fenly's possession,
Embarrassed her soul overmuch, and her ire

Took soberer hues, when the single-tongued fire
Found counter conduits, and redoubled diversion,
In ways too well known to have need of insertion.
One moment she scanned them, her breath coming fast—
Those witnesses beckoning the timorsome Past—
But quickly besieged by some vigilant thought,
Which oftenest comes when unsent and unsought,
She clasped to her lips the unsanctified lines,
Then twisted the leaves, like to one who resigns
Death itself unto death. But once in a life
We bury our dead out of sight. Husband, wife,
Lover, friend, for them all we may hopelessly mourn,
But one throb goes out with no tidal return ;
The wave that made empty, no waters can fill ;
No need of a grave on a far windy hill,
Or name writ in gold ; just as often abroad
Walks dark in the midst of the morning, the road
Alongside our own ; in religion's red light
Or the shade of the cross, still the lips may grow white ;
And never a river so calm and complete,
But has one shoreless place, where Eternities meet.

VIII.

Thus Mora interrèd her dead, nevermore
One echoing note from life's resolute score

Should cumber her ear ; so with unpalsied hand,
She cautiously gave to a perishing brand,
The letters, then watched, while the black wrinkles fell,
And covered the memory of Rupert Blondell.

IX.

Oh, hard are the lines of the man or the woman
Who writes of the passions of things that are human :
The letters are ashes ; Blondell smokes at ease,
And Mora may go and return as she please ;
The soft cheek of Persia is yet without stain,
And faint all the traces of tears that remain ;
And if Paul had died before writing this song,
There were no longer need this sad tale to prolong.

X.

But love and rebellion, revenge and regret,
With all their allies, in confusion are met,
And e'en so reluctant—some hand must unweave
The unloyal tissue,—therefore without leave
There may be presented in passing along
A certified copy of Fenly's love song.

XI.

TO MY LOVE.

My restless soul has climbed, how oft!
The shifting stairs of ecstasy,
To learn when pinnacled aloft,
How lone and lorn a height could be.

Times out of mind, I've strung my lyre,
To hymn some song in grander key,
Attuning to some soft desire
Or pent-up need of minstrelsy,

And felt the chords give, one by one,
Beneath the false, uncertain touch;
While through the melody would run
A thread of discord, overmuch.

Such songs of egoism born
I ofttimes sing, to hide despair;
Such songs, begot of hate and scorn,
More drear than sullen silence are.

But now the tangled harmony
I know; the shrinking lute's delay!
Because apart, afar from me,
The one key-note had slipped away.

*O Persia! rapture! not again
Shall soul so blinded, base, beguiled,
On wings self-builded, weak and vain,
Essay to soar, while thou, a child,*

*Trusting a destiny between,
Like threads, thy slender finger-tips,
Makes or unmakes a god, by e'en
The verdict of thy honeyed lips.*

*I dare not measure out my love,
Nor guess the power that sways my sense;
I only know if thou approve
All punishment is recompense.*

*Come, pale, sweet girl, and glide between
The darkening lines of one lone fate;
As primroses 'twixt summer sheen
And autumn winds, weird and belate.*

XI.

For which, with some subsequent notes in *addendum*,
They fitly might call on their saints to defend them—
The guilty, of course—since poor Mora's surprise
Was only excelled by her frenzy; her eyes
Shot addery tongues of unquenchable fires,
As hot and untempered as Fenly's desires;

And less well contained, being somewhat impromptu,
Although, for that matter, his lines were still damp, too,
From sweated impulses, in characters rude,
No passion complete, but has ways that are crude.—
However, she sought, at the dead of the night,
The couch he had chosen, since ever the blight
Fell over his life ; and confronting him there,
With all his heart's secrets made suddenly bare,
He quickly fell back upon recrimination,
Essaying to cancel his infatuation,
By charges of treachery, ending at length
With threats wholly shorn of significant strength,
By such *coup d'état* as one scarce need relate,
Having witnessed the pyre on the library grate.
But Paul wotted not, nor his aids and abettors,
The fate which befell the oracular letters ;
And Mora, with craft like the logic of lore,
Which leans for its lustre on something before,
Set seal on her lips, and most wisely resolved
To wait while the pith of the plot was evolved.
For witless albeit as Io and Zeus,
And unpreconcerted, all plotting or ruse—
Thus far at the least—between Persia and Paul,
Yet Mora, suspicious and learnéd withal,
As soon fill a sheet without postscript or blot,
As fancy a passion *sans* intrigue or plot.

CANTO X.

I.

How swift were the pen and how buoyant the verse,
  How phantom-like shadows of doubt should disperse;
How lustrous the line, and illumined the page,
How eager the soul every sense to engage
In rhythm and song, if but poesie's theme
Were chosen of scenes from some roseate dream,
Unveiled, unentangled, where love answers thought
In sinless assurance, unbidden, unsought,—
As odorous breezes, awaft from some shore
Antipodal, meet in ecstatic *rapport*,
And mingle in harmonied echoes.   Alas!
That into this record of foibles, should pass
The tainted and sooted impingement of wrong,
Less fair than icicles, less false than the song.
Yet so falls the light through the crimsoning stain,
And multiplied parts of the frail, fractured pane
Through which the world sees.   Who shrinks from the work
Of cleansing, may die in malarious murk.

Wouldst fetter a bird in his course to a star,
For shame that the wing wear captivity's scar,
While vultures in eager and carrion feast
Make havoc of prey which their greeds have increased?
Oh, countless the hearts, and the lives, have been laid
Prone, helpless, and futile, for lack of some blade
Courageous and cunning, to sever the knot
Of Gordian fibre ; to puncture the plot
Of cold malediction. 'T is well these poor lines
Have root in some truth, which redeems and refines
The lowliest task—so with cheerier heart,
Let us track the dark thread to its ultimate part.

II.

Now first, howsoever reluctant, the blaze
Enkindled of fagots, enmassed from the gaze
Of meddlesome, curious folk, lights the scene
With pitiless glowing ; and never a screen
Devised or so fashioned can shelter the head
Of Persia ; who, wiser, had builded her bed
Among the wet violets, over the hill,
Where only the thrush, or the sad whippoorwill,
And whitening stars should her threnody sing—
Out under the moon where the violets spring.

III.

Time swept down the columns of life, speeding fast,
And covered events with the dust of the past ;
But one thought stood picket in sun or in storm,
One name by soft lips kept unceasingly warm ;
That name was Paul Fenly, and never a pearl
Seemed purer to her than that name : foolish girl,
Guard thine own from harm. Ah ! How tardy to learn
That embers self-made are the embers that burn.

IV.

So Paul came and went, with the apple-bloom tints,
Just paling to white in his face, and the glints
Of sunlight and leaf in his autumn-brown hair,
With nothing of anguish and never a care
Writ down the soft lines of that harmonied face ;
While Persia forgot the despair, the disgrace,
The scorn with which cottage and salon were rife,
Forgot the wild vengeance and woe of a wife—
A wife in the eyes of the world just the same,
And all the world asks of a wife is the name—
Yea, even forgot the dull pain at the heart,
The slanderous word, and the answering smart ;
Forgot the misshapen and horrible cloud
With which her young heavens were immutably bowed ;

Forgot e'en the hour for her prayer to recall,
For dreams, in the opiate presence of Paul.

V.

Oh, where all that youthful and delicate charm
Of sense and of conscience, which catches alarm
At 'proach of a footstep forbidden of fate,
Or words too familiar, when whispered too late?
Oh, where the repellant, sweet sanctity fled,
That crowns like a halo the maidenly head?
Whence strayed the sweet accents of counsel, and where
Those reachless refrains of a mother's last prayer?

VI.

One answer in all; never attribute human,
Or law, or example of man or of woman,
Or prelate or priest, can e'er cancel the law
Which keeps worlds in place. But if wresting some flaw
From Polity builded of human decree,
Replacing for right, that which wrong seemed to be,
Then, social arbitrament may not imply
That marriage, unsanctioned by love, shall defy
All higher and holier law. First of all,
Whatever the verdict, such natures as Paul

More sternly severe readjustment demand
(And Paul not exceptional too) at the hand
Of some moral scourger, than any decree,
However distorted such edict may be.
Yet man's every error some truth underlies ;
And much benefaction is done in disguise.
Economy wisely distributes the forces
Which Nature, o'erstimulate, grasps at the sources ;
And those who make trips to Utopia, elect
To outlive their romance, and therefore expect—
Since social amenities fitly combine—
All hope of absolvement to promptly resign.
With logic like this, only one comment more
Remains to be made on this memorable score.
As soon should the sensitized agent resist
The light which He only " contains in his fist,"
As one by self-cautioning sense so unshielded,
Or one to perverseness and passion so yielded,
As Persia, with all the chaste conscience of woman—
A knowledge which rendered Paul's wooing inhuman
Beyond all known precedent—Somewhere in fine
In every man's sins should be found the white line.
So Persia, bewildered with leafing delights,
Thought nothing of days of gone bloom and of blights,
And dreamful, forgetful, and dreaming again,
Her moments of joy overlapping her pain,

Stood tip-toe, her new-found emotions to greet.
What wonder the world slipped from under her feet,
And left her alone in the sun and the wind?
Temptation before, dumbly seeing behind
The wreck of the ties she so carelessly broke,
She yet wove new tissues for whispering folk,
With every new morning.

VII.

There always will come
Some hour when our fears set adrift, gather home.
Some time more than others, when swart apprehensions—
Nurst well in their first-hood, but which, when dimensions
Crowd happier feelings, we jostle aside—
Return, reinforced: in such moments, our pride,
For once unrebellious, steals shrinking away,
And even our words we would gladly unsay.
Such hours came to Persia; the moon and the stars
Confiding, impulsive, looked in through the bars,
One warm stilly night, gilding newly the place,
And burnished a tear on the pictured young face.
She thought of the vow she had made months agone,
The vow she had sealed with the crest of the moon;
She thought how unkept those resolves, and how less
Than all, to her own heart, she dared to confess;

Then came the most blistering, withering pang
That fresh from the self-rebuked heart ever sprang;
A harrowing doubt, Ah! what famishing hope
Had caught the frail wrist leaning forward to grope
In shadowy places, and crushed it to pain?
Now first came the thought, how the rust and the stain,
From airs she had fanned, were corroding her life;
The ghastly suggestion that Mora, the wife,
Was outraged and wronged; that perchance, even Paul—
O traitorous thought!—had been plotting her fall,
And thus, a perfidious altar had builded,
Of honor and faith, with hypocrisy gilded!

VIII.

Now Fenly was bad enough, all the world knows,
And soulless, but wicked, as wickedness goes
In these days of license, is scarcely the name—
For faults too pronounced, for his passions too tame;
His sins shall be nameless; the best we can do
To shun the vexation—'t is charity too.

IX.

When woman gives rein to suspicion, no steed
Of subtle-bred fancy her own can outspeed;

Howe'er inconsistent, grotesque, unrefined,
All fancies find lodgment and place in her mind.
And Persia, like persons of sympathies fine,
Made haste to each pillar of faith undermine;
Till thoroughly wretched, and faint with despair,
She rose from her sofa, unloosened her hair,
And sank in the cushions, one scarce would believe,
More fit at that moment new faith to receive
Than ever before; 't is by such occult courses
Fate works out her will and her plan reinforces.

X.

An hour in the moonlight and silence alone,
Her slumber unbroken by even a moan;
Then sudden a tap at her drawing-room door,
And a shower of gas-light fell on the floor;
One glance at her pallor set Fenly astart,
And sent the hot blood chilling back to the heart,
As, poised like a Sappho in " Lesbian lights,"
She looked in his eye, from her self-imposed heights,
With critical, questioning glance, as dogs do,
Or children.

XI.

The man caught a magical view,
Clairvoyant or psychic, and straightway began
The breadth of each yawning abysm to span;

And even before the fair listener had spoken,
The thread of her anguish was virtually broken.

XI.

He said with much spirit, in musical voice,
That Mora at length had made rational choice,
And most unaffectedly, firmly preferred—
However distasteful the feelings that stirred
His heart for another—to order her table,
Her wine, and her wassail. In short, to be able
Her usual and special delights to pursue
(With all his resource in subservience too)
Unchecked, undeterred ; that her diamonds and dances,
Her houses and friends were her pleasures.
                                            His fancies,
She coolly assured him with greatest aplomb,
Could never disturb her, providing his home
And seeming relations continued the same ;
And ended by lightly declaring the name,
Won somewhat severely, she counted a gain,
And that, with his leave, she proposed to retain.

XII.

Poor Persia's young soul was steeped full in amaze !
'Mid all speculation, this singular phase,

Of selfish serenity, poise, or despair—
For words had no power to reach her just there,
If later—fell cool and refreshing like rain,
On cheeks parched with fever: it shut back the pain,
Displacing with feelings electric and rare,
Her doubts and suspicions, her gloom and despair;
Then sudden the brain grasped the terrible thought!
What destiny this, which these tidings had brought?
Some Scylla had risen as high as the world,
Where erst only Charybdis threatened and swirled.
What unseen caprice moves the womanly mind?
Where cross the dim lines of divergence?
          We find
To-day this girl's faith as sublime as the stars,
To-morrow distrust irredeemable mars
The simplest device; contrarieties meet,
And love unbaptized is itself incomplete.
So Persia's emotions grew icy or warm,
And swayed to the tempest, like masts in a storm.

XIII.

Dear child! if some pitying angel, this night,
With love such as we under orthodox light
Are fain to believe does, with whitest of hands,
Smooth gathering rimples, and strengthen the sands

Under infantine feet, could pause in its path
Of noondays and glories, and bring, not in wrath
But mercy, Remorse, to invite to reflection,
While reason gives conscience sublimer direction,
How merciful, mercy. Atonement, alas,
The sinner's resort, falls far short of the grace
And symmetry bred of a clean self-surrender ;
And how muchsoever her years may defend her,
This truth stands aloof—that the woman who feels
Her steps yield before her uncertain, who reels
Atilt on the banks of some limitless void,
May rest quite assured that the peace she enjoyed
Lies never before, and the sooner retraced
Her steps, the less sins to be later effaced.
However, no measure of morals, or grief,
Poured into this book, can avail; to be brief,
Paul Fenly—a husband—still waited and wooed.
She answered in accents she half understood,
With morals perverse, or with logic awry,
And which, or if both, one could scarcely descry,
And then in a breath, crimsoned hot to the brows,
As Fenly, ignoring his marital vows,
Planned future reprisals on destiny, showing
How easy annulment of marriage, bestowing
A much larger share of purport on a letter
To maintain a " fraud " than if he were better

Informed ; still bewildered, the shock of his words
Impaled with their sharp-pointed meaning like birds
Her thoughts on the wing, and so brought them to bay,
And left no decoy to invite them astray,
By glittering imagery, deftly outlined
Against the gray ground of a plan undefined.

XIV.

So, therefore, as hushed grew the din of the town,
And moons, less aslant, sent their messengers down
With maritime orders to put out the lights,
Paul Fenly went forth on this night of all nights,
With brain full of questionings ; not worldly wise,
Nor firm nor heroic he saw with shut eyes
How fit were persistence ; he knew passing well
How certainly intimate airs may dispel
Those finely-bred fancies, so daintily wrought,
Spun out from high purpose and disciplined thought ;
And carefully weighing her infinite love,
Gave tenderest trust to his powers to prove
His judgment profound ; and once Persia committed,
He boldly resolved to be never outwitted.
Paul Fenly, we may as well register here,
For once in his life was entirely sincere.
N. B. So sincere as a lover may be
Who mortgages that there is not—*non esse.*

XV.

Next morning Paul woke with a spring in his soul ;
His pillow was swathed in a soft aureole
Of russet and gold, like the head of the child
He loved and denied to the world ; so he smiled
In his weak, half-content, but quite summary way,
And promised his heart that the close of this day
Should weld his unlinked and unlicenséd hopes
With Vulcan-like grasp.
                 Meanwhile, as one gropes
Through dreams unfamiliar, impelled by some thought
Or fantasy fickle, his reveries wrought
All quaint combinations ; he clearly foresaw
That Mora proposed to hold fast to the law
Which made them as one—what remained if outdone,
If after the tournament honors were won
By Mora ? Above the pale spectre of fears,
Well kept in abeyance through all these long years,
So swiftly his fancy made disport and riot,
That even his questions and semi-inquiet
Fell idly behind in the fanciful race
('T were hard for the absolute sense to keep pace
With Fenly's romances) ; and thus by default
The problem stood in *statu quo*.

XVI.

To exalt
The virtues and beauties of Persia, of course
Was always a vital and affluent source
Of pleasure to Fenly ; he never recalled
The cost to the victim, so cunningly thralled
In meshes and webs, such as only a passion
Enweaved by his own fateful fingers should fashion.
And thus in sweet nothings, his mornings amusing,
He fairly succeeded in quite disabusing
His mind of immediate projects to mend
A rent in his life, or still further to end
The sad melodrama of sadder devise,
In unities faulty, adverse, and unwise,
Wherein he was playing promiscuous part
With dubious faith and more dubious art ;
But accidents thrive where a purpose will starve,
And even the hand that has failed to encarve
Laborious, for fortune or future a name,
Turns back to encounter both riches and fame.

CANTO XI.

I.

THE morning hours lengthened ; the town was astir ;
  The alternate spikes of acacia and fir
Spun out to a thread on the warm garden-wall,
And blent with the jessamine bloom, before Paul,
His toilet complete—not forgetting the while
That rarest exotic, the everglade smile,
Which lay in a sort of profusion among
The statelier lines of his face, as if sprung
Like wind-flowers in shade of the verdurous tree—
Turned his face to the world, with a conscience as free
As if there were never a heart to be broken,
Or never a " hail and farewell " must be spoken.
However, while dallying idly with Paul
That cleverest of women awaits in the hall
His matinal coming ; to quite intervene
The manly design and the woman's between,
She settled one hand, thus to emphasize bolder
Not too unpronounced, on the derelict shoulder.

II.

If stung by an adder, or maddened by pain,
Exquisite nor subtler had been his disdain;
She saw, and grew livid with rage and surprise.
'T was only a moment, but further disguise
Was impotent, useless; indeed the occasion
Afforded relief from all further evasion,
And lent him the courage he lacked by his will;
So urging the moment with greed, more than skill,
He fell on the letters, in parcel and part,
And squandered his fire with unsoldierly art;
Undreaming how feebly his utterances fell,
Continuing in words unambiguous to dwell,
With manifest menace and unequal stress,
On charges now needless to further express,
He ended at last, with sublime self-assurance,
Declaring their lives as beyond all endurance
Together with each—that 't were folly to waste
Two lives in atonement, for one hour of haste.
How better to grant each a final release,
Securing a life of inviolate peace—
That—biding such action—the proofs in his hand,
If honorably cancelled, were hers to command.
So ended.

III.

The woman had sunk in a seat
Embracing her figure, as if to retreat
Beyond reach of his words ; with lips firmly set,
Her basilisk eyes all unwarm and unwet,
How hard and unlovely she looked ! Yet the heart
Were stone, that unpitying witnessed the dart
Of sudden, unspoken, ineffable scorn,
And the smile grim and bitter, and wholly forlorn.

IV.

The pause which ensued was but brief. Mora spoke :
" I know well your purpose. Too weak to provoke
The prompt recognition your outrage invites,
Since lawfully wedded, my marital rights
I choose to retain—the reluctant release
You hoped to enforce in comparative peace,
You find quite impractical. Measures, therefore,
Made needful to further your latest amour,
Press close, and you fly to a 'bluff,' the resort
Of cowards ; my will to your manly resort,
However, I yield, with the single provision,
Which stated, shall wait your imperial decision.
You purpose my honor to coolly malign,
By charges as false, both in deed and design,

As hearts that conceive them. You never, from pen
Of mine, had in proof one such letter, and when
To attest it, you furnish one condemning line,
I promise all right of your name to resign.
And privileges, such as divorcement ensures—
Command you thenceforth—until then, I am yours!"

v.

Thus speaking, she pointed away to the door,
And drearily sank in her chair as before.

vi.

With haste more indecorous than blameful, mayhap,
Paul strode from the room, while the woman with wrap
Tight drawn to her quivering throat, sent a leer
Swift after, a leer wary, frugal, severe,
As if of her malice there scarce were enough
To eke out the ends of the half complete "bluff,"
Which now relegated to her clever art,
Allotting to Paul the subordinate part
Of victim.

vii.

With blank disappointment, and faint
And sick with disgust and dismay, the complaint

That rose to his white lips expired with a shock,
And never found utterance ; he turned in its lock
The impotent key, and then ran through his hair
His sensitive fingers, now cold with despair,
And, but that the nostrils were slightly distended,
All sign of his passionate anguish had ended.

VIII.

"You brought me the letters?" Her voice had a purr,
A *retroussé* inflect, like spikes of the burr
After frost time ; for now, though this triumph was won,
The old loveless life she had newly begun
Won fast on her sight. Fenly leaned on the slab,
Nor mindful of victories, satire, or stab,
All words in this moment supreme were the same,
Save that word were freedom, then—worlds for a name.

IX.

Spoke Fenly : "Where are they?—the letters, I mean,"
His accents were dry, yet his face quite serene.
But high in the chambers of vocal expression,
His voice seemed half strangled as if by compression,
As the note of an organ, when pent by the stops,
Through shadowy places uneasily gropes,

And strains at the keys in hard search of egress,
The over-fed passion of sound to express.
Thus Fenly in high and attenuate tone,
Half shrill and half plaintively spoke.
        Like the moan
Of wind out of darkness, behind her white lips,
More darkly portentous than cloud or eclipse,
A threatening retort kept the *tempo* between
His words and her own, e'en as chords intervene
In prelude or symphony. Guarded at first,
But gathering with unspent malignancy, burst
The storm in a wildly sown cyclone of words,—
Such only as pride deadly wounded affords—
Strewn random and recklessly, only intent
On filling the wide and impassable rent
With hissing *débris* from a mountain of scorn,
To blister his life, though it left hers forlorn.

.   x.

"Now drop the disguises of fawning regret
And phrases of 'would that we never had met,'
And pass to the gist of your meaning," she said,
In stifled retort to some soft and air-bred
Suggestion, too specious, too weak or refined,
To meet the full-angled misjoint of her mind.

XI.

"Let me go!" thundered Fenly, in sounds that approved
The infinite depth of the passion which moved
A soul unsustained, nor by license nor law,
Or civilized sanction ; which clearly foresaw
Two courses—one leading away through the gloom,
By ways more unwelcome than even the doom
Which faced at the ending the infidel soul,
Too strong to be led and too weak to control
As destiny willed ; and the other a stream
Like Tigris the river, which flows as a stream
Fast by, underground, the oracular grove
Where God walks—and angels, in Paradise—Love.

XII.

So slavish, so helpless, so bitterly shorn
Of power and self purpose, too ruthless uptorn
From unyielding tenets, for place in that school
Where "law is beneficence acting by rule,"
The words lost no meaning as moments went by
E'er Mora had gathered her wits for reply.
Then turning with features unlaxed from the leer
She wore in the first of the interview, fear
Nor craft now, nor pity, could throttle the hard,
Inflexible purpose, nor even retard

Its conquering course. "The time has arrived,"
She presently said, "when all that survived
Of feeling has turned to (I shall not say hate,
For that I could have for the dog at my gate)
A thirst most insatiate for vengeance ; nor even
The dread of the doomed, nor the hopes of a heaven,
Shall come between me and revenge, so beware !
For over the head of my infant I swear
So hot to pursue you with flood or with fire—
As well as the thing of your basest desire—
That nothing is left of your powers, your youth,
Your manhood or might, to attest to the truth,
That wooing and winning, and wearying soon,
Comprised your amusements from moon until moon.
Meanwhile, to your melodramatic appeal,
Words only my wholesome contempt can conceal;
If brought full to bay by such spurious schemes
As those you attempted, in which, as it seems,
You ignobly failed, the measures involved
Would rest on the possible verdict resolved
By society, namely : if dearer my fame
Or values accruing from owning your name,
A turn of the wrist has enabled me, sir,
To settle the question, and now I prefer
To hold you in bridle, for elsewise you might
Place some other woman in just such a plight."

XIII.

If this were a story of wrong and redress,
How simple and natural it were to express
Such comments, as tend the convictions to move
In minds half inclined to regret or approve,
Thus turning the balance one cause to sustain.
In fields before harvest, the full heads of grain
Take easy direction from lightest of winds,
While those standing upright are empty ; so minds
Well filled and well ripened, of growth most complete,
Take easy direction from thought. Like the wheat,
'T is only the minds which are empty or rotten
That errors retain, which are better forgotten.

XIV.

Society forges its hardships and wrongs,
Ofttimes with the consummate art that belongs
To womanly ways. On much the same block
It fashions her conscience, her stays, and her frock.
It teaches the tricks which it feigns to despise,
Shifts all its own sins on its victim's unwise
And unsheltered head, and with cowardly cringing
Conceals its own hand, while securing the hinging
Of gates once enpassed. Ignoring the woman
Who works for her bread, with becoming acumen

It makes recognition of such as elect
To barter a soul, if but with circumspect
And decorous seeming, by adding a clause—
However perfidious—embraced in the laws.
Then spreads its broad mantle in lewdish protection
On shoulders disfigured with signs of subjection,
And sneers at its votaries. Volatile, fickle,
It thrusts in the blade of its levelling sickle,
And mows down all merit, with merciless hand,
Save such as for uses its patrons demand.
There never was captive, and never a serf
On Ural's broad base, or Siberia's turf,
More surely the slave of the levelling yoke,
Than they who society's favors invoke
Above their own strength.
      Thus Mora surrendered
No jot of her pride ; if society tendered
Its verdict defending her fame—like the fetters
Of fate, shame was burned with the bundle of letters.

xv.

The interview closed with diatribes more
Pronounced and prolonged than hath profit to score ;
And, bowing more low than occasion required,
Paul turned to the door and so would have retired,

But Mora, with sudden transition of face,
Sprang up, and encircled his neck with embrace
In mood not unsimilar—so disconcerting—
To some savage ecstasy, wholly perverting
To womanly poise, and self sanctity ; whence
Inspired the pen, moved in pious defence
Of womanly rights, hewn of fallible stuff,
While woman her selfhood ignores ? Not enough
His contracts to spurn in the face of his faith,
Paul borrows her besom to sweep from his path
The relics of mutual pledges. In this
Most doubtful resort, what surprise he should miss
So unseemly aims ; he has failed in all sense
Of making a plausible, polished defence,
Before the all-judging society's eyes !
(None half so acceptable there as disguise).
Not enough that he sets up new idols in places
Where lingers in ground, fresh uptorn, still the traces
Of her unsteady feet ; not enough that these truths
Not even defended with pleadings of youth's
Imperative folly—but Mora can yet
So far the self-consecrate woman forget,
As dumb, to reclamber the slippery stair,
That hangs singly loft, in its sublimate air—
A guest most unwelcome, and thence to be hurled
Adown the bald heights in the face of the world.

How narrow the isthmus dividing the two,
Of love from self-love, of the false from the true!
A look of white scorn, such as Angelo traces
In Sistine Apollos with dumb scoffing faces,
Stood out for a moment against the dark wall;
Then only an echoing clang down the hall,
And Mora alone with her fate and her child,
Reflected a moment, then bitterly smiled.

CANTO XII.

I.

NEXT day every mortgage, conveyance, and deed,
    And monies to meet the insatiate greed
Of modernized social exactions, were filed
In favor and names of the wife and the child;
And Fenly, so far as the human heart knew,
Dispensed all the details in final adieu.

II.

Now moves the dull pen with unmanacled pace;
Now menacing fears cluster thick, to efface
With world-cunning finger, each fettering line,
And blot from the page each untoward design;
Now shrinks the weak flesh from the abatised road
So paved with sharp falsehood, with doubt so o'ergrowed
And tangled, that halting, uncertain, and sore
The feet that enlist for the lengthening score

Of measuring lives, illy judged, out of time,
Yet true to their moral strabismus. This rhyme
Makes record of truth; without plea or excuse,
It garners, unflinching, some sheaves, for the use
Of those who have witnessed the uneven thrust
Of blades so empoised every garlanded trust
To shear to the base; there is naught to recall;
Each heart knows its cry—there 's a God over all.

III.

And Persia took counsel of guardian nor friend;
She ordered her ways to subserve to the end
Of doubly refining each delicate sense
To justify fate to her feeling. Pretence,
Or coarse readjustment, or unreal life,
If shown in a flower, a woman, or wife—
With whimsical mood all too subtile for reason,
She daintily swept from her thought; out of season
With Nature too often, and oftener with art,
Her taste was the bitterest rival her heart
Ever found; with such sentient and sybarite fault,
No marvel her life was one scene of revolt
Of mutual rival offences; the hues
In somebody's gown, or the fit of the shoes,
The laces or perfumes, made index of mind
Esthetic, at least, if not ethic; refined

Discord fundamental gave far greater pleasure
Than harmonious sounds of tempestuous measure
From unclassic scores; so full of caprice,
Exquisite, perverse, as soon coalesce
The fires and the snows, or seek to make mate
Of nettles and lilies—or placate her fate,
As counsel with Persia.
     The pearl may be found
Well housed, and though captive, encompassed around
With friendliest tissues, yet lying apart,
Self-built, self-contained, sending fires from the heart,
Not fateful, like diamonds, but tenderer far,
Such lights as gleam from the cool reachless star.
As selfish, as sinless, as wilfully true
As pearls in their shells, or as stars in their blue,
Sat Persia apart from the world she defied,
Like one in the violet shroud of her pride.

IV.

Months wasted, and Time with its narrowing lens,
Brought focus and form out of doubt and suspense;
As shifted the tide, or the sands of the sea,
The verduous uplands of social degree
Kept tally with life; and still slowly the girl
Stepped measuredly out from the dance and the whirl,

And down through the mist of the plains where were
    glassed
In mirage some future too fragile to last,—
Some scene of enchantment, some phantom-lit tower,
Upbuilded in air and dispelled in an hour :—
So groped the blind path through the infinite wild,
The heart of the woman, the hand of the child.

v.

Sweet Sisters of Mercy ! what pæans of glory
Float down the long columns that record thy story !
How hushed grows the sob, how repentant the soul,
Entranced with the notes of thy pray'rful control !
No holier shrine than thy own sinless breast,
No emblem more pure ever spirit caressed,
Than altar of thine ; without folly or fault,
Thy choicest of wreaths for the erring are wrought,
And peace, in unstained and inviolate flow,
Makes music in hearts long attunéd to woe,
If bidden at thy sweet command.
                            Who shall sin
If guarded by angels of God ?   From within,
Each woman has light of her conscience ; the beacon
Tho' whelméd in passion, yet leads her to seek one,

Soft eyed and serene 'mid all worldly alarms,
And sweeter than sleep, the repose in her arms.

VI.

Such grace had been Persia's endowment in trust,
Which later she left to the moth and the rust;
But still like the roots of the *siempre viva*
—So deathless the faith of the early believer—
It lodged in the atticky haunts of her heart,
All dry and entangled, yet ready to start
From soil sorrow-fallowed, and moistened with tears,
So waiting in weakness through all the long years,
When bidden of anguish sweet Mercy uprose
From pious retreat, and from guardian repose,
And came at the call.   For weeks there had poured,
In hot malediction and menace, a horde
Of letters anonymous, shameless, and bold,
And impiously false and malicious. With cold
Disdain, not less bitter than helpless, the child,
Now reaping first fruits from the wanton and wild
And pitiless whirlwind, self-sown, turned away
Those barbaric shafts she was helpless to stay;
Committing, unbroken of seal, to the flame
All letters disguised in appearance or name.

VII.

As swift through her fingers one morning she passed
In bitter review some more kindly, she cast
A lingering, listless, and half-contained glance
At one superscription ; then swift as the lance
Descending, her hand with unquivering zeal
Seized firmly the missive, and tore back the seal,
To read in those characters dear to the eye,
Which naught, nor distraction nor time, shall defy,
That gentle, admonishing message of peace
And love, such as only the Sister Therése,—
With delicate eye, from the night-blooming stalk,
Along troublous ways, where the saints only walk
To bear up the weak ones—might single ; a balm,
An odorous herb, in the All-healer's name.
As reading—" They tell us the tree we have watched,
With measureless hope, has been blighted, o'ermatched
By early, devasting, insidious frost,
The bloom scattered wide."
                         With bare arms uptossed,
And fingers tight clasped in her soft shining hair,
Her agony writ in dark pencillings there,
She sat for long hours with poor, desolate face,
—Like a white rose forgotten in winter's embrace,—
Enframed in her arms ; and with far-straining sight,

She peered through the memoried shadow and light,
Along the dim way, where the Sister Therése
Led on to the foot of the Cross. But surcease
Of sorrow comes seldom by ways we approach,
And few are the chords which respond to the touch
Of fingers too joyless to waken the theme ;
As well make reality fathom the dream,
And filch its bright parts, as for peace to o'ergo,
With passionless pace, the abysses of woe.

VIII.

Paul came, and the sunshine stole back to her heart ;
She looked on the hours she had passed when apart
As spectral, or ghostly, unreal devices
To lure her from life and its joy; so entices
The passion which rests on a magnetic base.
So poiséd, this love, e'en the presence, the face
Inspires, reassures, and beguileth its victim,
So doubly intense that all powers of dictum
Are as naught against force. Then Persia began,
With careful observance, his features to scan,
If thence she might guess how his purposes moved,
And learn what new mode of defence he approved.
With always some cunningest " corner " on fate,

Paul tried Persia's varying hopes to elate.
And now with an instinct which sentinel-like
Stood high in the watch-tower of reason, to strike
With wisest of aim, at this obvious disguise,
Was Persia's intent; though his face, nor his eyes,
Wore ever more placid portent; yet, erelong,
As Persia had finished his favorite song,
He rose for adieux, in his sweetest of ways
Proposing an absence of many more days;
And then, before Persia believed she had heard,
Strode down through the lawn, and had quite disappeared.

IX.

Then followed those moments in life set apart,
Remembered when joy is forgotten; which start
As savages leap from the ambush, where faith
Had planned a secure and well-fortified path.
Those moments struck off from the meteor mass,
Which fall at the feet with dull sounds, such as class
With hours semi-conscious, yet leave on the brain
The stamps of a thunder-bolt.
      Persia, again
Slipping down to recover the letters that fell
As Fenly came in, felt a throb and a swell
At her throat and her heart; half convulsed she arose,

And reeling, she fell on a couch, in repose
More tragic than death, so dumb and so deep
The opiate madness, which counterfeits sleep.

X.

Ere Summer with fulness of days is complete,
While fields with unripened rewards are replete,
E'en yet, ere the briar, its bud and its bloom
Has yielded its sweetest, maturest perfume,
With a malcontent's grasp, and a mendicant's greed,
She leans forth to borrow the glow and the bead
From Autumn's exhilarant cup; not content
With pleasures too present, half garnered, half spent,
Yet wholly ecstatic, the leaf in the sere
Sheds tints unexpressed in the leaf more anear.

XI.

As Summer outreaching, so Paul Fenly's love;
Unvexed from impeding, untoward remove,
It languished; not fairly from morbid caprice,
But lack of some stimulant, fit to increase
And stay his voracious lust of himself;
Such lust as vain men reckon dearer than pelf,
And howe'er abundant the songs of his spring,
More affluent the melodies borne on the wing.

XII.

And Fenly came back, after many a day,
As full of soft greetings as mornings in May
Of sunshine and birds ; and Persia's young heart,
While filled with those harmonies, sadly apart
From common, concerted humanity's, beat
A dull yet distinct, undelusive retreat
Of hope for the future.
     If woman must err,
'T were Mercy that destiny timely defer
That vague and portentous presentment of ills
Which whispers unvoiced to her soul, and which fills
With mingled remorse e'en her measure of joy,
And amalgamates faith with the lead of alloy.

CANTO XIII.

I.

MEANWHILE, the shrewd Mora was working her will
With venomous zeal, and with masterly skill;
On some new device, each new morning arose,
On new schemes of vengeance, each night drew its close,
Till never tribunal, judicial or social,
But added its weight to the cruel sum total
Of sweet persecution. So follows the course
Of waters; what heed if defiled at the source?
Each aqueduct bears it resistless along,
Unmindful it sullies, with ruin and wrong,
White robes, dropped by fingers too weak for its sweep,
Untaught in the tricks of that ultimate deep,
Where social aquatics escape from the froth
Of slanders, beat up by the shallows. How loth
The world, though itself doubly doubting, to pause
And boldly give challenge to falsehood; because
The apple Eve ate was unsound, does it follow
That all the world's apples are found to be hollow?

But how muchsoever we court the conclusion,
Or seek to enmantle poor Persia's delusion
With down—as the eider bird lines the loved nest,
Fresh plucked from her pitying, contribute breast—
At one same tribunal all actions are brought,
And Mercy's triumvirate reckons for naught;
For Truth, Hope, and Charity only combine
The law to condone—not the law to refine.
And Justice has framed one Procrustean bed—
And fixes repose for the pillowless head;
One touchstone, high raised above logic or school,
As old as the world. 'T is the great Golden Rule
Makes easy the hardest allotments of life,
And draws from vexation its sting and its strife;
And never deliverance safer from doubt,
Than through those bright portals, encompassed about
With gloried assurances. Wherefore, O child,
Forsake the white way for the tangling, wild,
And encumbering shade? Is passion the soul,
And love its eternal and consummate goal?

II.

Undewy, and frowzy, and windless, and warm,
The morn in full western midwinter; the charm,
Half wrested from seas semi-tropic, remains

To fetter and fascinate dreamers. Who gains
A handful of life, gathered fresh from these shores
Of golden illusions, unfailing ignores
The vigors of soberer climes. Thus entwined
The life of young Persia with Fenly's ; his mind,
Exotic and sumptuous, swayed, as the breeze,
The grasses and greenlands, and low singing trees,
And willowy banks of the fanciful stream
Of Persia's sweet mental delights. So the dream
Grew real, the more the illusion, till woke
By the sharp, unexpected, and palsying stroke,
Like first guns in battle, and quick looking out,
Through varying mists of vexation and doubt,
The world seemed too strange, and too cold, and too wide
To succor her life, or to shelter her pride,—
And so came the end.

III.

One evening—no matter
That over the slippery pane, the soft patter
Of plenteous rain spread its translucent sheet
Of canopied mist upon pavement and street—
Two hands waxen white, fallen lax in her lap,
Two eyes, violet black, glaring wildly agape,
A look of dumb fear, such as seizes the fawn
When tracked from the forest she faces the dawn

On fields strange and leafless, made only such sign,
As bubbles on cauldrons of pitch. No design
Of pencil or chisel, in pigment or stone,
Ere felt the heart breaking, or measured a moan
From self-made abysses ; how therefore portray,
Through symbols so fashioned, the full sceptred sway
Of passionate anguish, so fierce that the soul
Lies pulseless and palsied and shorn of control?
That dull, chaffing check on reality ; what
Among possibilities laid to her lot,
In a life so ill-ordered, remains to lament,
Or sear her sick soul with more hot discontent?
Why only that Paul, in some bold calculation,
O'erstated the terms of his infatuation !
And only to show how unfettered the will,
Impelled by desire some new hope to fulfil,
The letter—escaped undeterred to the floor,
Now answering the breeze from the half-open door—
May furnish a key to the actions of Paul,
More accurate, fitting, and final than all
May else be submitted.

IV.

—And thus ran the letter :
"My own dearest one ! Surely you know me better,
And love me too well, after all these long years

Of trial and truth, be it sunshine or tears,
To doubt, or distrust, or condemn the reversal
Of acts more unwise every hour ; then rehearsal,
Of all we have suffered and sacrificed, proves
But profitless now : our unfortunate loves
Have borne their first fruits in such hot-house profusion
As spring from malicious, unchecked persecution,
And howe'er unwilling my spirit to yield,
Such wicked persistence has weakened my shield
Of self-sovereign strength. But to pity your fate,
My dearest, believe me, shall be the one great
And ultimate impulse of manhood's regrets ;
For who that once loves ever wholly forgets?
Yet you, with your subtile perceptions, may see
How perilous further persistence might be,
In fancies, which fade as we hold them too near
The sensitized plate of experience.
                                I fear
My words are inadequate, poor, and ill-chosen,
To fitly convey my best meaning ; a dozen
Of methods more novel I framed and rejected ;
Believing my motives should best be protected
By truthful exhibit—well knowing your mind,
And how toward generous thoughts you 're inclined.
This leads me, my angel, to make an allusion
To one phase of life which must cause you confusion.

Howsoe'er chaste your soul, or your purpose how high,
—And none know the poise with more surety than I—
The world is a glass whose mercurial test
Flings up but one side, for the worst and the best
And purity passes for that it may seem—
The proof of the coin is its power to redeem.—
So Persia, my love, it afflicts me to know
Whatever you do, and wherever you go,
One shadow must follow your sinless young feet,
Howe'er you advance, howsoever retreat.
Would heaven I could stay the unpitying hand,
A life should be writ in one word of command.
But pen shaped for power nor vengeance have I,
Nor courage, nor patience, to bear or defy;
Yet, though the whole world may be filled with contempt,
If your loving sanction but prove me exempt,
No care or concern more have I—and perchance
This only one love, this first, last, sweet romance,
May yet find fulfilment, by waiting the tide
Which two loving hearts it now seeks to divide.
If fate wills it not, and our foes shall survive
The wreck of their cruel misdoing, oh, strive
To cherish each memory sown in your heart,
And swear from your love for me never to part;
Only so I go back to that variable life,

Behind the fierce struggle to make you my wife,
Half solaced with thoughts that 't was I to inspire
A passion untiring through ice-fields or fire,
Which flows like one sea, with no backward intent,
Which knows no return till its billows are spent
In mid-ocean death. Think not life is shorn
Of all it held dear to you ; one blessed bourne
Remains, my beloved ; to the martyr-like soul,
The shade of the convent, the right to enroll
A name, which though sullied, may stand alongside
The whitest of saints who have suffered and died
For faith. Let the low, brooding wings of the Church,
Which sheltered your first orphaned childhood, still perch,
With vigilant eye, unrebuking and mild,
Above the flown bird it so loved as a child.
Nor yet unsustained by your sisterhood ; hosts
Of time-fretted frail ones reform, and the boasts
Of prelate and priest in their powers to awaken,
Owe much to those numbers whom vice has forsaken :
What more can I add, my lost love? every grasp
But strengthens the fetters we cannot unclasp.
For me naught is left but a desolate way,
Hemmed in by a law which I loathe, yet obey.
Ah, would that with you, love, to-night I could die !
But fate is our master,—good-night, and good-by."

V.

The signature here was reduced to a scrawl,
Unprecedent breach in the practice of Paul,
So clear, unconfused, and deliberate his pen,
So prompt in self-justification ; but when
'T is sought to explain, 't were unfair to withhold
One half or the other, the truth must be told.
Then briefly, and oh! for the shame of the shame
Of manhood, behind that hieroglyph name
Stood Persia's successor—
                          'T were otherwise better,
Mayhap, to unknit and unravel the letter,
As varying moods of biographers move
Their minds to excuse, what no mind can approve.
But nothing to bring anti-climaxes here,
Howe'er syncopated the time may appear,
It followed, as surely as pen may repeat,
Unmindful of unity, harmony beat,
That out of the furnace of Fenly's most dire
And fierce, but alas, unregen'rating fire,
Had risen new serpents his sense to beguile,
And catch ere it fell the half-trickeried smile,
Just fashioned and painted for Persia—Such sense
Must serve as the single and scornéd defence
Of Fenly's weak soul. Never rock that wave dashed on,

More pulseless than Fenly's unpitying passion,
Or empty of heart, yet he knew the world well.
With prophecies such as experiences tell
Against the sharp sound-board of life, he divined
The favored conceit, which, though cowering behind
The smooth-shapen fortress of honor—the trap
Where passion and prudence quite snugly o'erlap—
Carved out from men's conscience, such sanguine device
As further forbidden the further entice
His craven desires; therefore marriage, with men
Like Paul, much emasculates motive; and when
Society curtly confirms an amour
With nuptials—society votes it a bore.

VI.

But backward to anguish and Persia; no fold
How cunning and patiently wrought, though in gold,
Or Indian thread, like the web of the mist,
Or sumptuous, of substance unsparing, or twist
Of fabric, so proof against misery's might,
As safe to encompass poor Persia this night
From passion's wild tempest; and when at her feet
Her wraps fell unheeded, one only repeat
Made answer to storm from without and within,
Through lips white with anguish, "Lord, keep me from sin."

VII.

All night the wind moaned in unmeasured refrain,
And smote the wild boughs till they writhed in their pain.
All night the stark truth in enshackled control
Stalked down the dull pave of her dim-lighted soul,
Till low-browed, the dawn, with a menacing gleam,
Put by the thick shades; then, as up from a dream,
Slow rose the white figure, but staggered aback,
As glassing her features, the sullen and black
Recorder of woe stood defiant, in lines
Unblent with the whiteness that only defines
The shadows. One moment! now seized with a new
And horrible purpose, her eyes slowly grew
More widely astart; then as hunted from heights
Familiar, they fell, like the meteor lights
From heaven to earth's desolation, and grasping
The letter, she turned to her purpose, half gasping
An *Ave*—So plighted in childhood, how loth
The mind, to surrender the sign of its troth.

VIII.

Hangs never a sabre unseen in the air,
To strike down the arm which would hug its despair
To impetuous death? Was there never decoy,
Or mirage of promise, to trick out some joy

For span o'er the suicide's moment—or whelm
The hand of the fury misguiding the helm?
Oh! stay the frail fingers, and palsy the brain—
Too late! as the lips of the drunkard would drain
The last, most reluctant, and surfeiting drop,
The fate-impelled Persia steeps dumb her last hope
In dismal, defiant excess, with such zest
As only is lent from that cup labelled "Rest."

IX.

The end draws anear ; the last lurid glow
Of suns well-nigh set not infrequently show
Strange visions uplifted and hung for a season
In infinite air, with nor purpose nor reason,
Save only that life is behind. So await,
The vessels of bromide or mercury, the plate
Whereon is transfixed every life as it passes,
With equal and scrupulous sureness—the glasses
Or lens may be faulty, the chemicals foul,
But perfect the law which develops the soul.

X.

"Sweet Sister Therése" ;—thus wrote the mad girl,
"I question you hear me, from out the dread swirl

Where love lies engulfed. Let me see your white hand
Of pitying love ; let me hear your command,
To tighten my fingers in yours, lest I fall
In quagmiry places. How sharp I recall
Your sweet warning voice—but fate builded a way,
Over wimpling quicksands, inviting astray,
Eyes bred to the altar—and whence I had learned
Of " Him who all things overcometh," I turned
Obedient to love. I know how forbidden
The theme—I recall how ofttime you have chidden
My first faintest questionings ; now let the wild
Tempestuous breaker which swallows your child,
Perish full-voiced and spent at your feet. Only now
I write my first, last, indissoluble vow
Of faith to my own heart. If wicked or weak
At first, thrice accurst and impotent to seek
Repentance on narrowing altar or shrine ;
And if disaffected my heart, be it mine,
Its follies and aims and intents to atone,
In ways such as God and my conscience make known.
Some things must remain always dark to my soul,
Some unbidden doubts my dull reason control.
If love is adverse, wherefore Nature's decree ?
If nature is law, why shall laws disagree ?
If vital to-day, and to-morrow is fled,
What reckoning line 'twixt the living and dead ?

If love hide its face under mask of the law,
What wonder men seek for a fracture or flaw
To unshackle souls?—If faith is supreme,
What use of a plan to undo or redeem?
These harrowing thoughts too unsimple, confuse,
And give to conjecture those transporting views
Of love's immortality. Better my wings
Had beaten the bars of impossible things
To death, and despair, than this finding out,
Had cruelly borne me, high poised above doubt,
Across the broad seas, to this desolate shore,
Where my unburied dead quit my sight nevermore.
How great was my love, how unbounded my faith!
The winds in my face, or the thorns in my path,
Nor terror nor torture too sore, while in sight
I saw the strong torch of one passion alight.
It matters but little, the brand on my brow,
What verdict humanity renders me now;
Yet, holy of women! give ear, I implore,
My soul is as white as that morning of yore,
When smiling you kissed my poor orphaned brow
—How friendly that morning comes back to me now—
And fixed my young lips their first prayer to receive,
And taught them to murmur, 'My Father, forgive.'
The tempest is hushed; scarce a breath is abroad;
How near seems oblivion and respite: O God!

That women lag on, with their hearts in the dust,
Uptorn by some juggernaut wheel, from their trust
In manhood and truth; while the heavens are bowed
And pregnant with promise of rest. Let my shroud,
Enweaved as a bright revelation of truth,
Unvex the tired feet which unwisdom and youth
Have led in the by-ways of life. One thing more.
If, lifting "false keys" to the unopen door
Of scenes well concealed—if on oceans of doubt,
Where earth's swinging lamps shall have all gone out,
I venture my much crippled oars to dip,
Unsent and unsighted from shore or from ship,
What, tell me, sweet Sister, counts one more poor life,
One breath more or less in the sickening strife?
Whatever of time, of account, or of cost
Perversely I wagered and fatally lost,
The impotent title remaining in trust
Is scarce any more than a handful of dust,
To be sifted away on a shoreless sea,
Or washed to the beach of Eternity.
What angels have paved me a pathway of prayer?
Already I seem to be swinging in air;
The veil slowly rends, and new vision inspires
My unquickened powers with celestial fires!
Off, fetters of flesh! ye are loads to my feet!
How lovingly earth and the firmament meet!

Oh, joy ! all my worldly desires, one by one,
Like leaves winter-rotted, all outward are blown !
And now I can see, e'en on wings of such fleetness,
Uncovered the law, that all love is completeness !
O Angels—O rapture ! O faith ! one in three,
Bear me up, lest I fall—I am free, I am free !"

.   .   .   .

XI.

They lifted the form from the white marble stair,
And threaded the lengths of the sunniest hair ;
The shapeliest fingers they curved to their will,
And fashioned the eyelids, now stony and still ;
The violets, wet from the fountain's white crest,
They tied in a knot for her maidenly breast,
And the flowing folds of her creamy gown
They rumpled to rippling waves of down.
And over the heart that had ceased to beat,
They laid the pale Cross with its Promise sweet.

THE END.

www.ingramcontent.com/pod-product-compliance
Lightning Source LLC
Chambersburg PA
CBHW031349160426
43196CB00007B/787